MORE AUTHORS
AND I

MORE AUTHORS
AND I
By C. LEWIS HIND

Essay Index Reprint Series

BOOKS FOR LIBRARIES PRESS

FREEPORT, NEW YORK

First Published 1922
Reprinted 1969

LIBRARY OF CONGRESS CATALOG CARD NUMBER:
69-17576

PRINTED IN THE UNITED STATES OF AMERICA

TO THE READER

HERE they are, my fifty Men and Women Authors, arranged alphabetically, from Ade (George) to Zangwill (Israel). If, reader, you find some of your favourites omitted, please remember that there was a former book called *Authors and I*. This new volume, most of which was written in America, is named, naturally, *More Authors and I*. For I was allowed to acquire the habit of writing these studies, week by week, for *The Christian Science Monitor*, and as Mr. Frederick Dixon, then Editor of that excellent journal, liked them, and after *Authors and I* was published said encouragingly, " Carry on," I continued to write about the authors to whom I reacted, for some reason or another, at the moment, even such far-away figures as George Eliot and Herbert Spencer. And I am doing it still. For authors (and their vicissitudes) are many and persistent, and new ways of regarding them open unceasingly, like new dawns.

C. L. H.

Spring, 1922.

CONTENTS

Contents

MORE AUTHORS AND I

B

I. GEORGE ADE

GEORGE ADE is an American humorist.
I make this definite statement because
he is one by intention and by confession. It
is a new kind of humour to me: it is a humour that
is calculated, pursued, not genial, not kindly, rather
satirical, rather contemptuous, but it raises laughs.

At the dinner given by the Lotos Club of New
York to George Ade I was able to examine the
technique of his humour. He made a long speech
in response to the praises that had been lavished
upon him; and it was clear that his method is—
every sentence must arouse a laugh. It became
almost automatic. If the laugh did not come
immediately he reached a full stop, he would pause
the fraction of a second. The laugh always followed.

In one of the reports of this dinner the writer
remarked, "Mr. Ade gave away a lot of expensive
humour." I suppose that is so. The best humorists with whom I am acquainted so bubble with
humour that they cannot help expressing it even
when they are catching a train, or looking for a
collar stud; but it does not seem to come naturally
to Mr. George Ade and his kind. He looked quite
serious at the dinner. He might have been a
statesman or the president of a bank.

I cannot help thinking that his humour is manufactured, and he, being a very intelligent and

3

experienced man, who knows his public, and the
kind of thing that makes them laugh, can produce
a laugh-creating sentence at will. The sally that
aroused the loudest laugh in his after-dinner speech
was : " I built my country place in Indiana, not
to live in—merely to refer to."

Mr. Ade rose to affluence and fame on the Fable.
For twenty years he has been trying, so he says, to
escape from it. But he cannot. The American
public wants from him Fables, as it wanted puns
from Tom Hood, and marble from Alma Tadema,
as it wants serenity from Mr. Harding, and Home
Runs from Babe Ruth. The public knows exactly
what it wants.

I count myself fortunate that I came upon Mr.
George Ade's method of humour without knowledge
of it, and without prejudice. A year ago he was
little more than a name to me. If anybody had
asked me what I knew about him, I should have
answered : " A humorist of the west : one of those
who have helped to make Chicago the ' literary '
capital of the United States of America : an adept
in slang, who drives his points home with Capital
Letters."

One day, on a railway journey, I bought a copy
of an American magazine with a million or so
circulation. I looked it through, sampled it, found
the advertisements more interesting than the text,
and reminded myself what a large number of essays,
stories and poems there are in the world that I
do not want to read. Toward the end of the
magazine I found a page of Fables by George Ade.
This was a discovery. I read the Fables with

delight, finding in them a new method of literary expression; and although I did not know the meaning of all the slang words that this hard-headed, hard-seeing author employed, yet I felt that these Fables gave distinction to the magazine. The author had something to say.

I tore the pages out, intending to preserve them for the Portfolio I have kept for twenty years labelled, "The Best Things in Current Writing." And while doing so I decided that I would place them beside Crosland's Fables, which appeared in the *Academy* and elsewhere about 1900. The difference seems to be that Ade deals with Chicago, Crosland with Life.

I hope Mr. Ade will not call me an Elderly Grouch when I inform him that I have never been able to recapture the entertainment and the sense of novelty with which I read his Fables for the first time. The trick of them now seems obvious, the philosophy bitter, the slang forced. But they go on. The public is used to liking them. In volume form they have taken many names, *Fables in Slang* (the first), *More Fables, Ade's Fables, Hand-made Fables*. The last mentioned I bought, read through, and in conversation made the mistake of calling it "Machine-Made Fables." They have now grown very long. Crosland, like Æsop, would sometimes say his say in a few lines. Ade sometimes requires several pages, and although I am interested in the mechanics of them, I do not laugh as the fable unfolds. His machine runs very well : the object of a machine is to be efficient, not to express pathos, pity, or whimsicality. I still call his latest book "Machine-Made Fables." I wonder what Mr. Ade thinks of Barrie or Max Beerbohm. Modern American humour, as expressed by Mr. Ade, is rather hard. Compassion does not enter into it. It is metallic.

Am I wrong at not being amused? Ought I to laugh at this, a typical passage?

"The Peanut-Parlour of Pseudo-Art instead of popping like a Toy Balloon, according to Prediction, had absorbed a Gents' Furnishing Emporium and was blossoming out with a Double Front rivalling the Architectural Splendours of the Taj Mahal."

Or this—

"In a vast majority of cases she has not the Looks to back up the Title. Even the Buckingham Palace manner and the Arctic Front cannot buffalo the idle Spectator into overlooking the fact that she belongs to the genus Quince."

Perhaps I am wrong in not being amused because the publisher's statement on the jacket of *Hand-Made Fables* says : "Every story has a bright and shining point upon which some human foible of ours is transfixed. But it is irony that pricks without wounding, which recognizes that being sarcastic is a very human foible itself. Of course, it proves again that Slang is a fine art, and that humour distinctly belongs to American literature."

La! La!

But although Fables made Mr. Ade famous, and are his chief contribution to the literature of our day, he has gambolled in other fields. He has written a number of facetious books under such titles as *Artie, Knocking the Neighbours*, and he has

been a most successful writer of musical comedies,
and such-like things that run a year, and that give
the " frivolous playgoer " snappy sentences to
remember and to quote. I am informed that " I
feel like thirty cents " comes from the George Ade
mint.

It is curious that the two expressions of Mr.
George Ade's abounding talent that have most
interested me are my first encounter with him and
my latest. The first was that reading of his Fables
when they were quite new to me : the latest was
his autobiography, published not long ago in the
million or so circulation magazine that has taken
him under its wing. The very title of this autobiography made me smile. It is called *They Simply
Wouldn't Let Me Be a High-Brow*. To that is
added this sub-title—" Those ' Fables in Slang '
which I began to write twenty years ago started
me upward on my dissolute career and landed me
in the gutter of notoriety."

It is a most humorous autobiography, and, as a
contribution to a History of Journalism in Chicago,
most valuable. It is a romance of " getting on."
For a long time Mr. Ade had been writing a column
called " Stories of the Streets, and of the Town,"
and after ten years of " clanking toil " had worked
his way to a salary of 60 dollars a week. One
morning he said to himself—" Why not a Fable for
a change ? And instead of slavishly copying Æsop
and La Fontaine, why not retain the archaic form
and the stilted manner of composition and, for
purposes of novelty, permit the language to be ' fly,'
modern, undignified, quite up-to-the-moment ? "

The Fable was written. It was about Sister Mae and her sister Luella, "whose Features did not seem to know the value of Team Work." It caught on. It clung on. More followed, and Ade fell into the arms of " the wizard who sold syndicate features to the daily press." Soon he was getting 800 dollars a week and later " passed the thousand mark."

" Can you beat it ? "

America is a great country. Such a thing never happened to George Meredith or Thomas Hardy.

And yet, throughout this delightful Autobiography, which is perhaps the best thing George Ade has written, there is a note of wistfulness, or regret. He harps on the Great American Novel : he hints playfully that had he not been so Tremendously Successful in a Side Show : had not the Syndicate Wizard been so clamorous for More Fables he might have—

Who knows ?

There may be more than meets the eye in that title—*They Simply Wouldn't Let Me Be a High-Brow.*

When I said to my neighbour at the Lotos Club dinner : " Why did they give this signal honour to George Ade ? " he did not answer, but turned to his companion and asked, " Why is George Ade our guest of honour ? " Another pause. Then a man behind, who had overheard the questions, replied, " Because he's George Ade."

Literary Fame is a queer Jade. Lord Dunsany has written a little play about Her.

II. JAMES LANE ALLEN

IT is no reproach to an author to find himself in the ten-cent, or even in the five-cent box. This fate happens to all. Libraries are dispersed, an unbookish man inherits the family volumes, folk move to another town; then the second-hand book dealer, in an untidy suit and with benevolent eyes, makes a ruthless and absurd offer for the lot, and is ready with his sack or his cart.

However I may be hurried, I can rarely withstand the temptation of the ten-cent box. Sometimes it is a sad experience. No one likes to see his friends drop down in the world, through no fault of their own, but through the chances and changes of life. Such an experience I had in New York, when, on my way to see a sunset from Staten Island, I missed an Elevated or two, because I paused to look through a ten-cent box which I had not investigated recently. In the box I found *The Choir Invisible* and *The Heroine in Bronze* by James Lane Allen.

While the Elevated ground down to South Ferry, and while the steamer glided across the bay, I dipped into *The Choir Invisible* and recaptured much of the rapture with which I read it, so long ago as 1897. What a charming story it is, so sane, so wholesome, so full of a kind of interior beauty and high-mindedness; and what a happy picture it

9

gives of life in Kentucky nearly a century and a quarter ago. I remembered the beginning—" The middle of a fragrant afternoon of May in the green wilderness of Kentucky : the year 1795."

I remembered, too, that when *The Choir Invisible* reached London in 1897, I reviewed it with fervour, and I almost started from my seat on the Staten Island boat, when I read, in the publishers' advertisements at the end of the book, an extract from the review that I wrote in 1897. Here it is : " A book to read, and a book to keep after reading. Mr. Allen's gifts are many—a style pellucid and picturesque, a vivid and disciplined power of characterization, and an intimate knowledge of a striking epoch and an alluring country." Since those days *The Choir Invisible* has done well—very well. In 1901 it was in its 223rd thousand. Everybody who reads has read it, and enjoyed it.

Having renewed acquaintance, so pleasurable, with Amy, and Mrs. Falconer, and John Gray, and John Gray II, I turned to the other book by James Lane Allen that I had picked from the ten-cent box—*The Heroine in Bronze*. What a disappointment ! It did not hold me at all; it did not interest me, and when I turned the pages and found this sentence—" And now, before the Shears of Silence clip the threads which have woven this piece of life's tapestry and are near the margin of the canvas, etc., etc.," I put down the book and said—I'll read no more.

This book does not come off. It is sentimental; the writing is too fine, overlaboured, and the characters are idealizations; they are not drawn from life. Mr. Allen is a man of ripe sentiment, prone to fine writing, and with a tendency sometimes to think that he is standing in a pulpit, not sitting at a desk. He, like everybody else, has the defects of his qualities. In *The Choir Invisible* he held his defects well in hand, and he was controlled by his deep-seated affection for his beloved Kentucky; but in *The Heroine in Bronze* (it was written fifteen years afterwards) he wandered away from life into a kind of sentimental dreamland, which no doubt he felt to be real enough, but of whose reality he has not been able to convince at least one reader.

Then I thought of *The Kentucky Cardinal*, one of his earlier books, and said, That surely is in the class of *The Choir Invisible*, because in it he deals with Kentucky, and when his native state is his theme he is at his best. I recalled it (my copy has delightful illustrations by Hugh Thomson) and remembered the book with pleasure; remembered also the ripe humour that runs through it, in the style of, but less sophisticated and more mature than, *The Dolly Dialogues*. And there was the sequel called *Aftermath*, in which sentiment quite gets the upper hand, and which allows the author, at the end, to indulge in the luxury of grief.

While I was watching the sunset from a hill in Staten Island, and the ships passing to and fro in the Narrows, I reflected how the fashions in literature change, and wondered if people still read this serene, uplifting and lovable writer, who has seen new generations of authors rise up and catch the public; and who, in the passage of years, has become more of a preacher, which is quite natural, and less a teller of stories with a meaning. He was never wholly a novelist : he has always had something to say which is more important than the vicissitudes of the relations between men and women.

I am sure that he is at his best when dealing with Kentucky, and my investigations, when I returned home and went through his books, fully confirmed this. That comedy in letters, an outside of Kentucky volume, which he calls *The Emblems of Fidelity*, is well done, but it is too remote : this outpouring of a literary and well-stored mind, with a turn for humour, is of the study and the brooding scholar. So is *The Bride of the Mistletoe* and its successors. These books glide too easily, and as for *The White Cowl*, which someone has extravagantly called " the finest short story in American fiction," I find it merely insipid.

Of the Kentucky books I like also *The Reign of Law*, in which he actually makes the story of hemp fascinating; but for interest give me *The Kentucky Warbler*. That is a book to remember, a book of place, a book that sings of nature. And there is the volume called *The Blue-Grass Region of Kentucky, and Other Kentucky Papers*. If I were asked to choose three representative books by James Lane Allen I should select those loving and informing *Kentucky Papers*, *The Choir Invisible*, and *The Kentucky Warbler ;* and could I resist adding a fourth, *A Kentucky Cardinal* ?

From an interview with James Lane Allen by Isaac Marcosson I learn that most of his books were written in New York hotels. When his friend expressed surprise at this he answered, " The question is often asked, how can a man in a city write of a country far away that he has not seen for years ? But that country is never far away and the man looks over into it unceasingly. He has but to lift his eyes to see it—as clearly as he does the people in the street."

To all men their home and their homeland are so stamped on memory that no after experiences, however vivid and varied, can efface them. It has long been my idea that the social, yes, and religious and political history of America, can best be told by taking each state as an entity ; and I am glad to find that Mr. Allen has this feeling also. It is his opinion that, " The serial of the nation must be told in terms of its states. Each of these states is a little entity all its own. Together the story of their lives and individualities comprises the larger narrative of the country."

From this consideration of the literary work of James Lane Allen it should not be difficult to sum up, in a sentence, his contribution to the history of his time. Let me try. How will this do ?— " He gave romance and reality to Kentucky."

Even in the ten-cent box I see and scent the blue-grass region of his waking dreams.

III. "F. ANSTEY"

AUTHORS may be divided into four classes: those who are eternally successful; those who are very successful for a time; those who have a spasmodic spurt of success, and those who never have any success at all.

"F. Anstey," or, to give him his correct patronymic, Thomas Anstey Guthrie, is in the second class. He was very successful for a time. *Vice Versa*, his first attempt at authorship, published in 1882, when he was twenty-six, was prodigiously successful. So was *Voces Populi*, issued in 1892. He has published many other books, but in the ideal library, which I sometimes have in mind, these are the two that I should select to represent "F. Anstey."

Careful librarians insert the word Guthrie after Anstey on the title-page. When he published *Vice Versa*, he had been lately called to the bar, and I suppose he concealed his real name lest litigants should think that a humorist is not the proper person to win a lawsuit. But he need not have worried: he soon gave up the bar, commenced author, and joined the staff of *Punch*.

When I wrote that "F. Anstey" belongs to the "very successful for a time class" I was not forgetting his contributions to *Punch*. There for years he was continuously successful. The humorous articles signed " F. A." have been read by thousands, by generations, for *Punch* readers are faithful, and they drop into the way of regarding a favourite humorist as an inevitable humorist, and laughing regularly. As George Grossmith once said : " They laugh as often when I do serious things as when I do funny things."

But in spite of " F. Anstey's " contributions to *Punch*, and the fact that he published a book in 1915 called *In Brief Authority* (it escaped my notice), it seems a long time ago since he flourished : since the days when everyone was talking about *Vice Versa*, *The Tinted Venus*, *The Pocket Ibsen*, *The Travelling Companions*, *Voces Populi* and *The Man from Blankleys'*, which was made into a most amusing play. How does " F. Anstey " stand to-day ?

Two courses are open to me when I wish to discover how the present generation is receiving an author who was once very successful. I talk with the girl librarians at my favourite New York Branch Public Library, and I consult Mr. Smiles, the most affable bookseller in Manhattan, who has every author of any kind of reputation catalogued in his mind.

There are nearly twenty " F. Ansteys " on the shelf at the Branch Public Library, but the cards pasted within the covers show that the demand for them is not brisk. *Vice Versa* has had many readers since 1917, but *Voces Populi* does not seem to attract the New York public.

When I consulted Mr. Smiles about " F. Anstey's " popularity he was inclined to be uninterested. Mr. Smiles is actual, or, as he expresses it, " up-to-

date." But he thought he might have a copy of
Vice Versa.

"Humorous," he remarked, putting his fingers
to his brow in the attitude of remembrance, "very
good humour."

"Yes," I replied, "very good eighties humour.
An enthusiastic notice in the *Saturday Review*
made *Vice Versa* famous. If you can disentangle
a copy from your shelves I suspect that you
will find the pith of that review quoted in the
advertisements at the end."

Mr. Smiles found the volume, somewhat shop-
stained, and this is what we read—

"The *Saturday Review* says : ' If ever there
was a book made up from beginning to end of
laughter, and yet not a comic book, or a " merry "
book, or a book of jokes, or a book of pictures, or a
jest book, or a tomfool book, but a perfectly sober
and serious book in the reading of which a sober
man may laugh from beginning to end, it is a book
called *Vice Versa : or a Lesson to Fathers*. . . .
We close the book, recommending it very earnestly
to all fathers in the first instance, and their sons,
nephews, uncles, and male cousins next.' "

Mr. Smiles rubbed his hands. " That's the kind
of review we booksellers want," he said. " I wish
American reviewers were more appreciative, more
—er—excited. They seem afraid to praise. Ah,
' F. Anstey ' is now a back number."

"Come, come, Mr. Smiles," I said. " If you
can't sell an author that doesn't show that he's a
back number. How about *Voces Populi* ? "

Mr. Smiles reflected a moment. " Was it not a

biggish, square book with a lot of italic type in it
and illustrations by Bernard Partridge ? "

I smiled and nodded, smiled because Mr. Smiles
is so true a bookseller : he remembers a book by
its size and look, and the artist who illustrated it.
" Did you ever meet Mr. Anstey Guthrie," he asked
suddenly.

It was curious that Mr. Smiles should have
addressed this question to me, because I was at
that moment recalling a walk I had once with
" F. Anstey."

" I met him, Mr. Smiles, at a dinner-party in
Kensington given by a publisher in the early
nineties. Those were the days when the humorous,
dialogue story was popular, and the conversation
that evening turned on this lively form of literary
journalism. ' F. Anstey ' was making a hit with
them in *Punch*, and Pett Ridge was also amusing
us with his humorous dialogue stories in the *St.
James's Gazette* and the *Pall Mall Budget*. He
took Anstey as a model, I suppose, but his dialogues
were not copies : indeed Pett Ridge had a richer
humour, and riper sentiment, and sympathy for his
Cockney creations. Opposite me at the publisher's
dinner-table was a short, fresh-coloured youngish
man, rather silent ; indeed, I don't remember that
he spoke at all. But his was an intelligent silence.
His eyes twinkled behind his glasses, and his quick
movements of attention were often more eloquent
than words. Well, the dinner and the after talk
passed as usual, and when hat and coat time came I
found that the silent, amused man and I were going
in the same direction. I beguiled the way by

c

continuing the humorous dialogue-story talk that
had cheered the dinner-time, and spoke freely of
the merits and demerits of the method, illustrating
my argument by criticizing the examples that were
appearing in *Punch*. My companion helped me
to talk, fed me with a spoon as it were. When we
parted I felt that I had been saying too much, but
rather neatly, and to the point."

Mr. Smiles shouted with laughter. "Your unknown companion was the author of *Voces Populi*.
Ha! ha!"

"That was so," I answered. "I discovered it
later from our host, the publisher."

As Mr. Smiles's shop happened to be free of
customers I removed a pile of *The Outline of History*
from a stool, and seating myself said, "You might
find it interesting, Mr. Smiles, to make a study of
the technique of the Anstey dialogue-stories in such
collections as *Voces Populi* and *The Travelling Companions*. It is an amusing form, and in the hands
of a master like ' F. Anstey ' is very readable, but
I think it is more welcome as a sip in weekly pub-
lications than as a deep draught in a book. Study
' At a Dinner Party ' in *Voces Populi*, Mr. Smiles,
and you will get the Anstey method to a T. His
long books are a different matter. *Vice Versa* and
The Giant's Robe are based on Ideas, and Ideas as
you know, Mr. Smiles, are rare. *Vice Versa* is
really an unforgettable book. Why don't they
include it in ' The Modern Library '?"

"Ah," said Mr. Smiles, shrugging his shoulders :
that "Ah" meant, "I am only a bookseller,
but——"

To be quite sure of the standing of " F. Anstey " I called at a palatial book establishment on Fifth Avenue and asked if they had any books by " F. Anstey." The manager (I always call him that) reflected, " Anstey, Anstey ! Ah, his *Vice Versa* had a large sale many years ago, and I seem to remember some call for his what was it ?—Baboo, Bayard from Bengal or something like that."

The manager addressed himself to the telephone, calling up, I presume, the vast, dim chambers where books are stored. Then, turning to me he said, " We have nothing of ' F. Anstey's ' in stock."

Some authors are very successful for a time.

.   .   .   .   .

LATER.—When I returned to London I had the good fortune to meet " F. Anstey " again. He no longer writes : he now devotes himself to art, his old love.

IV. WILLIAM ARCHER

WE met again in New York and talked of old days and old friends; and of new days, new movements and new plays. Also of his play.

He told me, in strict confidence, the title : that he had come to New York to discuss the play with Winthrop Ames, and that he would return to America in the autumn for the *première*. " And remember," he said, " that it isn't laid in India, but in an imaginary country beyond the Himalayas."

I promised to remember. A pause while I watched this tall, sturdy, book-and-lamp Viking.

Recalling that he had made a study of the Negro problem and written a book on it called *Through Afro-America*, I told him of the latest development —the proposed return of the Negro to Africa. He smiled; but I saw that he was not interested.

" That was a good book of yours, Archer," I said, " on *Poets of the Younger Generation*. What I liked about it was the absence of emotionalism, or ecstasy. You examined these young poets as you examine the Negro, or Ibsen, or a play by Shaw, or Mr. H. G. Wells' idea of the Deity, or a National Theatre : you bring to anything you study the rugged detachment of your Scandinavian ancestry."

" I'm not a Scandinavian. I'm pure Scotch, born at Perth. I have lots of relations by marriage in Norway, and I know the country, but I am not a Scandinavian. My father was of Queensland, Australia."

" You have also translated Ibsen, have you not ? "

Being a Scotchman, he smiled, and I, to recall the conversation to a becoming seriousness, said, " Have you seen Drinkwater's *Lincoln*? "

His reply interested and delighted me. This veteran who has seen every play of importance since 1879, when he became dramatic critic of the London *Figaro*, and has written about most of them, said, " It impressed me as much (I think he said more) than any play I have ever seen. The New York performance is much better than the London presentation."

A further pause. " This is rather like a ' Real Conversation,' " I said. " Another of your books that I liked was that called *Real Conversations*. You gave a new form to the Interview and I wonder that it has not been adopted oftener. George Moore's Conversations with Edmund Gosse were rather Georgemooreish. I fancy he introduced a good deal into Mr. Gosse's mouth. Now I am quite sure that all your Conversations were authentic reports. No one would suspect W. A. of inventing or indulging in any kind of whimsicality in a ' Real Conversation.' " He looked as if he agreed with me; but he made no answer. Another pause.

" What have you been doing since I last saw you —when was it, in 1915 ? "

" During the war I did war work. I was appointed to the Ministry of Information. There I wrote pamphlets and articles and a small book,

you know it—*Gems of German Thought.* I had
another war book ready, but the armistice made it
unnecessary."

" And since ? "

There was no need to ask that question. Relieved
of war work he turned with zest to an enterprise
to which all dramatic critics, I believe, secretly
aspire. He wrote a play. His thoughts are full of
it. It was his interest in this play that made him
rather indifferent to my comments on the excellent
books he has written. Long ago he proposed to
write a play with Bernard Shaw. That was
Widowers' Houses ; but " Shaw took the bit between his teeth, and made it all his own." The
new Archer play was to have been in collaboration
with Bernard Shaw, but this time, I gather that
Mr. Archer took the bit between his teeth. He
wrote a scenario so full and complete, that Shaw
said, " It is mere laziness to ask me to collaborate
with you."

" I hope that your play will have as great a success
as *Lightnin',*" I said.

He gravely acquiesced, and departed to keep an
appointment with Winthrop Ames.

When this Scotsman, who translated and introduced Ibsen to England, had gone I opened his
Playmaking : a Manual of Craftsmanship, and spent
an hour with that clear-sighted, logical, informative
volume. Archer's prose proceeds the way Ibsen's
characters talk. The characters say exactly what
they mean, and the listener absorbs the meaning
exactly. So with Archer's prose. He thinks before
he writes ; he is never in a hurry, never lyrical or

rhetorical, and the even beat of his sentences and clauses express the even beat of his thought and judgment. If a Rolls-Royce engine could speak I suppose that it would converse in the way that Mr. Archer writes. But he also has a restricted Scotch humour, not flaunting, but apparent to the perceptive. This treatise on *Playmaking* begins— "There are no rules for writing a play." As to his more explicit humour I have seen ironical verses by him, not as good as W. S. Gilbert, but better than I could write.

He is very serious in his writing, and quite scholarly and painstaking. I am now going to quote a passage from *Playmaking*. It is rather long, but it will show the reader the trend and temper of his literary method. You will find it in the chapter called "Dialogue and Details." The author has been saying that "The most destructive fault a dramatist can commit, in my judgment, is to pass, in the same work of art, from one plane of convention to another." To this he appends the following footnote—

"Mr. Israel Zangwill, in his symbolic play, *The War-God*, has put blank verse to what I believe to be a new use, with noteworthy success. He writes in very strict measure, but without the least inversion or inflation, without a touch of Elizabethan, or conventionally poetic, diction. He is thus enabled to use the most modern expressions, and even slang, without incongruity; while at the same time he can give rhetorical movement to the speeches of his symbolic personages, and, in passages

of argument, can achieve that clash of measured
phrase, against measured phrase, which the Greeks
called ' stichomythy '; and which the French
dramatist sometimes produces in rapid rapier-play
with the Alexandrine. Mr. Zangwill's practice is
in absolute contradiction of the rule above suggested that blank verse, to be justified in drama,
ought to be lyrical. His verse is a product of pure
intellect and wit, without a single lyric accent. It
is measured prose; if it ever tries to be more, it
fails. I think, then, that he has shown a new use
for blank verse, in rhetorico-symbolic drama. But
it is no small literary feat to handle the measure as
he does."

Of course he has written a book on America (we
all do), with a section on " The American Language," which begins—" Nothing short of an
imperative sense of duty could tempt me to set
forth on that most perilous emprise, a discussion of
the American language."

I pass this section. Mr. H. L. Mencken's eye is
on us.

I turn from the present to the past, to the day
when I first met William Archer. It was evening,
an evening in 1889, and the occasion was the first
performance of Ibsen's *A Doll's House* at the old
Novelty Theatre in London, with Janet Achurch
as Nora. William Archer and Bernard Shaw sat
just in front of me. So impressed was I with this
play (Ibsen was new to me : he opened the gates)
that I went the second night, and again on the third
and fourth nights. And I am under the impression

that both Archer and Shaw were present again and again.

W. A., so he signed, was then dramatic critic of *The World*, and it was chiefly through him that the English stage became, in part, intellectual and educative. He raised it. Now, like Fanny, he has written his first play, and you may be sure that if I am within a hundred miles of New York I shall be at the first performance.

.   .   .   .   .

LATER.—I was anxious on the first night of William Archer's play, *The Green Goddess*, when it was produced in New York.

I was anxious because this is William's First Play, and I could not help recalling the literary men—Thomas Hardy, Henry James, George Moore, Joseph Conrad—who have essayed the stage, and who have not triumphed. Lo, before the end of the first act my anxiety was over. I turned to Belinda and said, " This is all right." At the end of the second act I said, " This is a money-getter." At the end of the third act I said, " Archer has put it over." At the end of the fourth act I cheered with the rest.

This play is the work of a craftsman. The author of *Playmaking* has demonstrated his theories, and has had the courage, not common among Intellectuals, to keep his feet on the ground and his head away from the clouds. But the play has atmosphere, and it gains enormously from the exquisite acting of George Arliss and the perfect stage setting of Winthrop Ames. Mr. Archer should write an

epilogue chapter to *Playmaking*, under the title,
" How I did it." Critics are requested to note,
and to remember that the scene is not laid in India.
The action passes in " A remote region beyond the
Himalayas." Those who are acquainted with the
ways of the British Censor are aware how important
it is to insist that the Archer-Arliss " Raja of
Rukh " is not an Indian potentate.

STILL LATER.—*The Green Goddess* ran for nearly
two years in New York. W. A. was sixty-five when
The Green Goddess was produced. There is hope
for us all.

V. BERNHARD BERENSON

UNTIL last month we had never spoken. He was remote. I caught sight of him in the old days—now and again—in his hurried visits to London, a dapper man, vivacious, observant, attentive, a quick and inspiriting talker, rather an æsthete, not in the least like the typical 100 per cent. American. (He was born at Wilna, Russia, and educated at the Boston Latin School, and Harvard.) I do not suppose that he ever wore a belt, or left off his waistcoat, or that he plays golf with President Harding.

Although he visits America occasionally, spending much of his time studying Italian pictures in American collections, his home is near Florence; and whenever I have been in Italy, I have always had the half purpose of going out to Settignano and calling upon him. Probably I should have been welcome, as I have said nice things about him when reviewing his books, and he told me the other day, when we met, that he liked what I had written about him, and was grateful. I never called on him at Settignano, I was always pressed for time, or something silly; but one day I said over to myself the opening lines of Browning's " Time's Revenges." They are not entirely apropos, but

27

there is a flash of a recognition of our case in
them—

> " I've a Friend, over the sea ;
> I like him, but he loves me.
> It all grew out of the books I write ;
> They find such favour in his sight
> That he slaughters you with savage looks
> Because you don't admire my books."

In a way the last two lines are apropos, for I have
again and again defended Berenson's art theories
and demonstrations among my over-critical art
friends. There are, alas, so many experts who let
their disagreements with an author blind them to
the gratitude they should feel for him, like the
man who could not see the great beauty of Brooklyn
Bridge because, in his opinion, some of the rivets
close at hand were unsymmetrical.

Bernhard Berenson is one of my favourite authors
because I am immensely interested in art, and
because he has added immensely to my knowledge
of art, and has led me patiently, persuasively and
with ardent discrimination through the rich history
of Italian painting. What does it matter if I do
not always agree with him, or if I cannot
always follow his line of reasoning ? He himself
changes as his connoisseurship broadens and deepens,
and he is not afraid to acknowledge a change of
mind, or to indicate a deeper insight.

Doubtless, to-day, he would not write a book on
Lotto with quite the admiration that he expressed
in *Lorenzo Lotto : an Essay in Constructive Art
Criticism*, published in 1895. That volume has

been misunderstood. It was not a book in praise of Lotto : that not-very-great painter was used as a motive for a disquisition on the Methods of Art Criticism. He says in the preface to *The Study and Criticism of Italian Art :* Second Series : " Instead of an abstract discourse on Method, I thought it wiser to exemplify method in a concrete instance, and wrote my *Lotto.*" The unlearned in art should turn to *The Study and Criticism of Italian Art :* Second Series, and read the last essay on the " Rudiments of Connoisseurship," which the learned and buoyant author calls " A Fragment " of a book that has not yet been written to be called " The Methods of Constructive Art Criticism." Herein are set down the rules by which the advanced school of connoisseurs judge a picture, apart from its æsthetic import and communication, which to the picture lover are the things that matter. But the connoisseur is keen on correct attributions, and Mr. Berenson notes that the formal elements in judging a picture are divisible into three classes.

" The most applicable : The ears, the hands, the folds, the landscape.

" The less applicable : The hair, the eyes, the nose, the mouth.

" The least applicable : The cranium, the chin, the structure and the movement in the human figure, the architecture, the colour, and the chiaroscuro."

There is not an essay in these three volumes, the First, Second and Third Series in *The Study and Criticism of Italian Art*, that I do not find of

absorbing interest, the work of a man who loves art,
who has devoted his life to it, who is fearless, and
who never plods along the obvious beaten track;
but I am quite prepared to find some of my friends
who are interested in art, but ill-informed about it,
regarding these essays on a first perusal as " a bit
tough," such people as my Manhattan acquaintance
who said to me point-blank over a dinner-table,
" Say, sir, what is the difference between Corot
and Watteau ? " Such as the Virginia gentleman
who, thinking to please me, murmured, " When I
go to London I make a bee-line for Landseer."
And there is the Staten Island dame, who paints
a little herself, and was troubled because she could
not find the life of " Amico di Sandro " in Bryan's
Dictionary of Painters and Engravers.

That was amusing, because " Amico di Sandro "
is a fictitious personage, an Anonimo (see the essay),
imagined by Mr. Berenson, who imitated Sandro
Botticelli, who may have been his friend, and who,
under Mr. Berenson's ruthless and constructive
criticism, becomes a credible person with a number
of pictures to his name. The end of the essay is
as good as a Sherlock Holmes *dénouement.* Amico di
Sandro being established, suddenly a real painter
leaps into the narrative, with characteristics like
those of Amico di Sandro—one Berto Linaiuolo—
and, says our connoisseur, " Amico di Sandro may
be the historical Berto Linaiuolo." I wonder the
American Sunday newspapers never reached out
for this story.

But the best essay for the general reader is that
on Leonardo. I delight in this piece of work,

because it is so honest and straightforward (Mr. Berenson calls it a re-valuation); but it chagrined those good people who are always hurt when somebody tells what he believes to be the truth about something they have accepted, because it is easier to accept than to examine. Mr. Berenson quietly, subjectively, exhaustively dethrones Leonardo—and he gives his reasons. This formidable re-valuation begins, " As a boy I felt a repulsion for Leonardo's *Last Supper*. The faces were uncanny, their expressions forced, their agitation alarmed me."

How much I owe to his four little books called *Venetian Painters of the Renaissance*, 1894; *Florentine Painters of the Renaissance*, 1896; *Central Italian Painters of the Renaissance*, 1907; *North Italian Painters of the Renaissance*, 1907. My copies are thumbed and scored. These books are ideally planned—half illuminating essays, half lists of the authentic pictures by the painters discussed. There are no better guides to Italian painting, its beginning, its growth, its flowering, than these books, and herein you will read of " tactile values," a phrase that has been so widely discussed in art circles (" to realize form we must give tactile values to retinal sensations "), perhaps too widely, for long afterward Mr. Berenson had to explain that " tactile values " is only one element in a picture, that there are others, that there is " spiritual significance," so obvious that he took it for granted the reader would recognize its existence without undue stressing.

Again and again in his books he mentions his " master," Morelli, who really began the modern

method of connoisseurship, measuring the eyes, ears,
lips, etc., seeking accuracy of attributions from the
rule that painters do not vary materially in their
drawing and modelling of eyes, ears, lips, etc. But
the author of *Venetian Painting in America*, his
latest book, has more heart than Morelli, and the
pattern and insight of his essays have a deeper
philosophy.

I met him under ideal circumstances. It was
in the New York apartment of Mr. Carl Hamilton,
the young man who made it the purpose of his
life to own some of the finest examples by the Old
Masters. I went round them with Mr. Berenson
as guide—Cimabue, Bellini, Botticelli, Piero della
Francesca, Mantegna—to name but five. It was
a great art adventure—unforgettable. And I have
met him, too, in a gallery, here and there, for it is
something for a modern artist to persuade Berenson
to look at his pictures. On one of these occasions
the young painter who was holding a one-man
exhibition rushed up to me as I entered the gallery,
with outstretched hand, crying, "Are you Mr.
Berenson?" I gave him the answer that I gave a
voice on the telephone, who, when I was living in
Westminster, after a lot of ringing, demanded if I
was the House of Lords. In each case I answered,
"No!"

I am confident that I am not too enthusiastic
about Mr. Bernhard Berenson, whose art enthusiasm I began to hear about soon after his
Harvard days. That some people in the busy
world are also enthusiastic is shown by a page of
Vanity Fair, which I have preserved. It is

called " We Nominate for the Hall of Fame " : it contains five portraits, and one of them is " Bernhard Berenson—Because he has written that splendid series of books on Italian art which light our way across the museums. . . ."

VI. ROBERT BRIDGES

WHEN, in 1913, it became necessary to choose a new Poet Laureate, the voice of England clamoured for Rudyard Kipling. I do not mean to say that there were meetings in Trafalgar Square, and fugitive riots; for the Man in the Street is much more interested in his breakfast, in catching his morning train, and in preparing to earn his daily living, than in helping to choose a new Poet Laureate. Moreover, the office is rather laughed at, for although it has been held by men of genius, it has also been held by mediocrities; and the mere idea of any connection between Poetry and Officialdom would make, as Andrew Lang might have put it, a cat laugh.

But the Man in the Street in England, although he may not read a line of poetry from one year's end to the other, is conscious of the past; he enjoys a Tradition or even an Abuse if it does not interfere with his habits. He likes the Lord Mayor's gilt coach, the mature Beefeaters who guard the Crown jewels, the black ties that all naval officers wear, and the notion of a Poet Laureate, for there the abstract becomes a concrete concept, which is what the Man in the Street understands.

He also likes the verse of Rudyard Kipling—from "Recessional" to the "Absent-Minded Beggar"; from "What Do They Know of England, Who

34

Only England Know" to the "Barrack-Room Ballads"; and when he gave any consideration to the question, "Who shall be the next Poet Laureate?" naturally he said, after a brief mental consideration of the very few names of poets he knew—"Why, Kipling."

That was the opinion of most people, except, of course, the Government official or the officials whose duty it is to advise the king on the choice of a Poet Laureate. These functionaries want a safe man, not necessarily the best man, but one who is pleasing to certain interests, and who will not shock or disturb anybody. A William Cullen Bryant will always be chosen, never a Walt Whitman.

Of course all highly cultured persons in England knew all about Robert Bridges, including his contemporaries at Eton, and Corpus Christi College, of which he is an Honorary Fellow; also many Oxford dons, active and passive; and his companions at St. Bartholomew's and the Children's Hospital, from which he retired in 1882 to devote himself, I presume, to the Muse. But the Working Journalist knew little more about him than the Man in the Street.

So when the news was flashed through the United Kingdom and Ireland, to the dominions beyond the seas, and to America that Robert Bridges had been appointed Poet Laureate (some Americans, I am told, thought that the recipient of the honour was Robert Bridges, editor of *Scribner's Magazine*) there was a great searching in reference books for something to say about the new Poet Laureate. That day the British Working Man read, or probably

his wife spelled it out aloud to him, that Robert
Bridges is author of various plays and poems,
including " The Growth of Love," " Prometheus
the Firegiver," " Eros and Psyche," " Nero,"
" Palicio," " Ulysses," " Christian Captives,"
" Achilles in Scyros," and " Demeter, a Masque " ;
also of *Essay on Milton's Prosody* and a *Critical
Essay on Keats*.

The writers on the weekly journals, who are
sometimes better informed than those on the dailies,
and who certainly have more time, turned to *The
Oxford Book of English Verse*, and finding nine
poems by Robert Bridges in that excellent anthology
(Francis Thompson has one poem only) were able
to present to their readers a tolerable statement of
the Poet Laureate as Poet. They were able to
quote—

> " Love, from whom the world begun,
>   Hath the secret of the sun.
>   Love can tell, and love alone,
>   Whence the million stars were strewn. . . ."

And—

> " Whither, O splendid ship, thy white sails crowding,
>   Leaning across the bosom of the urgent West,
>   That fearest nor sea rising, nor sky clouding,
>   Whither away, fair rover, and what thy quest ? "

And—

> " The hazy darkness deepens,
>   And up the lane
>   You may hear, but cannot see,
>   The homing wain."

But these are just the beginning of Robert
Bridges, the few poems that have crept into an

anthology. Oh, there is also that fine, stalwart thing, which he calls " Johannes Milton Senex," beginning—

" Since I believe in God the Father Almighty,
    Man's Maker and Judge, Overruler of Fortune,
    'Twere strange should I praise anything and refuse Him
    praise. . . ."

This is the only poem by himself which the Poet Laureate has included in his Anthology—*The Spirit of Man*.

You see I am making the best case that I can to assure you that Robert Bridges was the right person to be Poet Laureate. But do I succeed? His longer poems, his dramas and his masques, have the look of Poetical Works, and they conduct themselves just as Poetical Works should, but I will present a new hat to anybody who can assure me that he has got to the end of " Prometheus the Firegiver "; " Demeter, a Masque "; and " Eros and Psyche "; or any of the others, even the thirty and more pages of " The Growth of Love." Certain sweet girl undergraduates, with golden or other hair, must be quite familiar with " Demeter, a Masque," because, on the title-page I find this— " Written for the Ladies at Somerville College and acted by them at the Inauguration of their new Building in 1904."

I fear, however, that Robert Bridges, as Poet Laureate, is a disappointment to the Man in the Street, for the simple reason that he expects the Poet Laureate to signalize every important national event with a poem in *The Times* on the morning after it has happened. Rudyard Kipling can do that. Robert Bridges cannot. How often, during the war years, on the morrow of some Victory or Home-coming, or Thanksgiving, did I hear the Man in the Street say, "Why doesn't the Poet Laureate butt in?"

And yet I am coming to the conclusion that Robert Bridges is entirely the right kind of Poet Laureate. He does not strike the lyre in honour of the retirement of Mr. Warner from active cricket, or for the home-coming of the Prince of Wales; for his muse is cloistral, classical, and gentle and does not cotton to acclamations and events. But he has done much in other ways; he has, against odds, held the citadel of good breeding in letters, and he has striven to uphold the purity of the English tongue. I need only remark that he is the originator of the Society of Pure English, and author of that pamphlet of constructive idealism, *The Necessity of Poetry*. Above all he is the compiler of *The Spirit of Man*. That was his war work, done in the darkest days. It gave, and is giving, heart to many. Knowing all this I submit that a man can be an excellent Poet Laureate even if his muse does not become vocal at the call of the daily press. Perhaps it is better to aid the mission of poetry than to write poems.

Many of our vocal poets might read with advantage that section of the Works of Robert Bridges called "Poems in Classical Prosody." Here speaks a cunning and loving artificer who understands what great poetry is, even if he cannot often make it. I must copy out a portion of one of them. It is

called " The Fourth Dimension " and under it, in
parenthesis, and in italics is the word (Hendeca-
syllables) :

> " Plato truly believ'd his archetypal
> Ideas to possess the fourth dimension :
> For since our solid is triple, but always
> Its shade only double, solids as umbrae
> Must lack equally one dimension also.
> Could Plato have avoided or denied it ?
> So Saint Paul, when in argument opposing
> To our earthly bodies, bodies celestial,
> Meant just those pretty Greek aforesaid abstracts
> Of four Platonical divine dimensions."

The man who wrote this could hardly have
written the " Absent-Minded Beggar."

VII. EUGÈNE BRIEUX

TO me the "Institut Français du Royaume Uni" domiciled in London is a novelty. It has appeared, since I was in London last, in Cromwell Gardens, South Kensington, "En face du 'Victoria and Albert Museum.'" In driving past I saw the French and British flags flying outside the gaunt building, and wondered what the "Institut Français du Royaume Uni" might be.

I was told that French men and women of letters, famous politicians, poets, dramatists, and others lecture there, the aim being to make English people more conversant with French thought and vision. Some kind person began to send me tickets for the "Conférences," chiefly on French painting and poetry, but I did not attend; oh, because listening to a lecture in the French tongue, even with refreshments and a reception to follow, does not draw me like steel to a magnet.

But one day I received an invitation to a "Conférence Spéciale" at the "Institut Français du Royaume Uni" that drew me to the magnet. Indeed, I broke an engagement to attend. The attraction was this: Monsieur Eugène Brieux, de l'Académie Française, the famous French playwright, was to lecture on "La femme française dans mon théâtre." There were also other attractions. Mr. A. B. Walkley was to preside, and

Mr. Bernard Shaw had promised to move the vote of thanks—Shaw and Walkley, perhaps the two acutest minds in England, old friends, but also old antagonists about the kind of propagandist literature that Brieux practises.

I am fairly familiar with the thesis plays of Eugène Brieux, and the literary warfare that has raged around him. *The Three Daughters of Monsieur Dupont* was produced by the Stage Society at the King's Hall, London, in 1905; *Maternité* in 1906; *False Gods* at His Majesty's Theatre, under the direction of Sir Herbert Tree, in 1917, and so on. My attitude toward the thesis play is quite simple. If it is well done I call it a good play, and recommend it to my friends. The plays of Brieux and Bernard Shaw interest me extremely, and when critics urge that the discussion of social problems should be confined to argumentative books and the high-class magazines, I answer—" Why ? " Those who do not like thesis plays can stay away from the theatres where they are performed. We who like them, and who profit by their dialectic, should be allowed to see them in peace. In this matter I side with Mr. Bernard Shaw rather than with Mr. Walkley. The difference between them, in its simplest elements, is this : Mr. Walkley wants to be entertained in the theatre ; Mr. Shaw wants to be instructed.

Then there is Mr. Arnold Bennett.

My excellent memory recalled a short essay by Bennett on Brieux in his lively volume of dogmatic pronouncements called *Books and Persons*. This brief Brieux essay was written in 1910. It begins :

" I foresee a craze in this country for Brieux."
Mr. Arnold Bennett then proceeds to warn the
English people that Brieux isn't worth twopence.
That is Mr. Bennett's way, and whether I agree
with him or not, I find his method stimulating and
amusing. Here are a few extracts from Mr.
Bennett's Brieux article :

" Brieux is a man of moral ideas. . . . He is a
reformer and a passionate reformer. But a man
can be a passionate reformer, with a marked turn
for eloquence, and yet not be a serious reformer.
. . . I have not seen one of his plays which I could
refrain from despising (with the exception of *The
Three Daughters of Monsieur Dupont*). . . . It is said
that Brieux's plays make you think. Well, it
depends who you are. . . . Nothing can keep
Brieux's plays alive ; they are bound to go precisely
where the plays of Dumas fils have gone, because
they are false to life. I do not expect to kill the
oncoming Brieux craze, but I will give it no quarter."

There ! That was Mr. Bennett's opinion some
years ago. I do not suppose that he has changed.

Now the decks are getting cleared for action.
Scene—the peaceful " Conférence Spéciale." In
the centre Monsieur Brieux, on one side, Pan-like,
Bernard Shaw, on the other side courteous and
careful A. B. Walkley, supported (far away) by the
unbending, vehement, inflexible Arnold Bennett.
It would have been perfect if Mr. Bennett could
have been persuaded to move a vote of thanks to
Mr. A. B. Walkley. But nobody can persuade
Arnold Bennett ever to make a speech. As to the
audience, there was the French Ambassador, a

sprinkling of lords, a large number of well-dressed amiable and appreciative Frenchwomen and English-women, and a few men, Intellectuals, I am sure, who looked, as they always do on these occasions, as if they were a little surprised to find themselves in such a gathering.

Also, there was Mrs. Bernard Shaw (Charlotte F. Shaw) sitting modestly at the back of the platform. She has had a hand in the English fame of Brieux : indeed I believe that she began it.

On my table reposes a book with this title— " *Three Plays by Brieux.* With a preface by Bernard Shaw. The English Versions by Mrs. Bernard Shaw, St. John Hankin, and John Pollock." The title-page does not mention the inclusion of a Foreword by Mrs. Bernard Shaw, in which she describes how during the winter of 1906–7, she became possessed of a copy of *Maternité* by Brieux, and how, when she had finished it, " I felt an event had occurred, and a new possession came into my life." I can imagine Mrs. Shaw and Bernard talking it over, growing more and more enthusiastic as morning after morning Mrs. Shaw through that " chilly winter and spring " strove to make the translation " as perfect as I could." Then, when it was at last finished, and two other plays included, the volume was published in 1917 with one of those long prefaces (forty pages) by Bernard—forthright, acute, Shavian—analyzing and applauding Brieux —" the only French dramatist whose fame crosses frontiers and channels, and fills the Continent."

Also on my table lies another volume of trans-lations of plays by Brieux—*Woman on Her Own,*

False Gods, and *The Red Robe*, with a preface by
Brieux himself, memorable for this confession—
" *La Foi* (' False Gods ') is without a doubt, of
all my plays, the one which has cost me the most
labour and the one upon which I have expended the
most thought and time." The end of the preface
by Brieux is this : " The problems which I have
studied I am sure I have not brought to their final
solutions. My ambition was to draw and keep the
attention of honest people on them by means of
the theatre."

As far as I can gather the difference between a
" Conférence " and a lecture is that at a " Conférence " the speaker sits. Monsieur Brieux sat
informally at a table in the centre of the platform,
and Mr. Bernard Shaw and Mr. Walkley erect, and
very wide awake, on either side of their distinguished
guest. Erect and wide awake ? Because they were
on guard. Mr. Walkley knew that Mr. Shaw, in
his speech, would chaff him. Mr. Shaw knew that
Mr. Walkley would make sly allusions to his thesis
drama propaganda. And Monsieur Brieux, knowing
no English, would not have the slightest notion of
what either of them was saying.

It all turned out beautifully, and just as I had
expected. Monsieur Brieux, who is now clean-
shaven, and looks as Mr. Asquith did some years
ago, defended Frenchwomen from the aspersions
of French novelists, and read portions of his own
plays in support of his argument. His address was
a perfect example of the way such things should be
done—intimate, intriguing, with just enough action.
It was the art of the " drawing-room " theatre

transferred to the platform. I understood most of
it, or some of it, and when I was at fault, Belinda
at my left, and two ardent Frenchwomen in front
"put me wise," until our neighbours cried "hush."

I might have understood more had I not been
engrossed in watching the faces of Mr. Shaw and
Mr. Walkley, making mental points ; and seeing, in
the mind's eye, the scowl on the face of Mr. Arnold
Bennett at this adulation of Brieux. For Mr.
Walkley in his speech was so courteous and Gallic
that the Man in the Street, if by chance he had
strolled into the "Conférence," would have been
amazed were he told that Mr. Walkley had ever
yawned at a Brieux thesis play.

Mr. Shaw, in his speech, was just himself. In
ringing tones he commended and applauded Brieux,
comparing him with Hogarth, inasmuch as Hogarth
in painting, and Brieux in playwriting, are originals,
and invent their own technique to meet their
needs. He also told the audience that, in the
French drama, there was no great creative figure
between Molière and Brieux. And he congratu-
lated Mr. Walkley on the evidences of interest he
showed, on this occasion, in having his mind
improved.

In their speeches both Mr. Shaw and Mr. Walkley
regretted that shyness prevented them from making
their remarks in French. I determined that Monsieur Brieux should know that one Englishman, at
least, in the audience could overcome the affliction
of shyness. So, at the reception that followed,
when I was wafted into the presence of this distinguished Frenchman, and presented to him, I

said, with deliberation, pronouncing each word carefully : " Monsieur Brieux, j'ai reçu beaucoup de plaisir de votre conférence charmante."

As we retired from the Presence I said to Belinda— " Didn't I do that well ? "

She gave me a look which may have meant—" I am proud of you."

VIII. A. H. BULLEN

WAS A. H. Bullen a typical scholar? If I were writing a novel, which needed a scholar as a leading character, should I explore my memories of A. H. Bullen and use him as a basis? I do not think so. He was not at all like the typical scholar accepted of literature and drama. Yet he was a real scholar; but he was also something else. He was a poet at heart, and also in act to a small extent. For there lies before me a little book of fifty-four pages, called *Weeping-Cross and Other Rimes*, a posthumous volume, with a photograph of himself as the frontispiece, seated in his house at Stratford-upon-Avon, against the entrance to the garden. He is reading a folio; his great " fluff of hair " catches the eyes; and somewhere near to where he is sitting is the Stratford-upon-Avon Printing Press, which he founded, and where he printed his great Shakespeare, and so many other fine editions of Elizabethan and Restoration poets and dramatists.

One of his dreams — this Printing Press at Stratford-upon-Avon—came true. He had been fired in 1903 with the ambition to print and publish a great edition of Shakespeare's Complete Works in the poet's native town, and so he acquired a lease of the house of Julius Shaw, the friend of Shakespeare, and the first witness to his will. In this house, two doors to the north of New Place, from 1904 to 1907, the type of the ten volumes of the Stratford Town Shakespeare was composed by Stratford men.

Bullen wrote, mostly in pencil, the Notes to the " Shakespeare Head " edition of the Sonnets, a beautiful volume, with a Foreword by Mr. Brett-Smith about Bullen, touching upon the life of this poor but rich scholar, who was so beloved, and who has created for himself a record as an " incomparable editor of old plays," the re-discoverer of lost or forgotten lyrics, and a student of English literature who never faltered in his task. He achieved much ; he planned much that he did not achieve ; and students and lovers of our English tongue and literature will be glad to know that the Shakespeare Head Press is to remain, in a large way, Bullen's monument. The directors of the Press announce that they " are anxious that it should produce no work unworthy of its traditions, whether in scholarship or in printing ; and it is with full appreciation of the handing on of the torch that they issue, as their first publication, the final word upon a literary problem of universal interest of the great scholar whom they succeed."

This " first publication " is *Shakespeare's Sonnets,* a beautiful book, the cover a blue, foliate design, the page noble, and simple. The " literary problem " is, of course, the problem of the Sonnets, the identity of Mr. W. H., and the Dark Lady, and the various inaccuracies of the text, which such famous editors as Dowden, Thomas Tyler, George Wyndham, and H. C. Beeching have tried to

elucidate. In seven pages of Notes Mr. Bullen
sets down a lifetime of study of this subject. If
you desire to have an object lesson in the way a
Shakespearean student works, procure this book from
"The Shakespeare Head," Stratford-upon-Avon,
or from Basil Blackwell, Oxford, and read Bullen's
Notes. Here is a specimen : "Though some of
Shakespeare's Sonnets are difficult to interpret and
a few are so cryptic as to baffle the most searching
inquiry, it must be allowed that the text of the first
collected edition—the 1609 quarto issued by Thomas
Thorpe—is fairly free from serious corruption.
George Wyndham went so far as to suggest that
Shakespeare himself saw the first edition through
the press. . . . If Shakespeare read the proofs his
carelessness passes belief. Again and again ' thy '
is misprinted ' their.' Generally we can correct
these misprints *currente calamo*, but in two instances
the reading is doubtful. In Sonnet XXXV, 8, the
quarto gives—

> " ' Excusing their sins more than their sins are.'

"Malone (following Capell) changed ' their . . .
their ' to ' thy . . . thy '; Wyndham reads ' thy
. . . their '; and I have ventured (diffidently) to
print—

> " ' Excusing " their sins more than thy sins are." ' "

There you have the Scholar condensing into a
quarter of a page months of reading and reflection.
As may be imagined, scholarship, as a way of earning
a living, is not as lucrative as being a movie star.

E

I suppose it is the worst paid profession, and Bullen failed even to obtain " that usual reward of the English scholar, the honourable poverty of one of our greater Universities." There may be a dozen people, hardly more, who are excited by a learned new edition of Anacreon, or a Variorum text of Beaumont and Fletcher. Such things are not " money-getters," and so Bullen, faithful to his love, and ministering to her year after year, could not help being troubled and embarrassed financially. He longed to see Greece, to travel there with his friend George Gissing. " But poverty held him tied at home, and all his voyaging was done on winter nights by his own fireside, when he would devour books of travel with the lusty appetite of a schoolboy."

I knew him best, and saw him oftenest in the days when he was associated with Mr. Lawrence in the firm of Lawrence & Bullen. They had offices on the ground floor, a large area, divided into many rooms, at Henrietta Street, Covent Garden. When *The Studio* was started I persuaded Messrs. Lawrence & Bullen to allow us the use of the two front rooms overlooking the street, and so it happened that at odd hours of the day I would stroll down the passage to the partners' room of Lawrence & Bullen and discuss—anything. Lawrence sat at one end of the mahogany, manuscript and book-littered table, Bullen at the other. Lawrence was sometimes out, Bullen was always in, and always with a pipe in his mouth and a book before him, and always a book that was a hundred or more years old, and always he had a smile of welcome for me.

From this firm issued, in peacock blue and gold, the delightful Muses Library—Blake, Gay, Marvell, Drummond, Henry Vaughan, Herrick, Waller, Donne, Carew, Browne—a set of which I bought some time later when it was " remaindered." It was early in those days for beautiful, scholarly books. The Public had hardly begun to acquire them. Bullen was a pioneer, not a money-maker.

Do you know John Masefield's description of A. H. Bullen ? " I saw him under two conditions : the one in London, where he was always among scholars and writers, in rooms in the Inns of Court, or in dark supper-rooms in the Strand, talking of Elizabethan books and people much as though they were alive in the streets outside, like the time come back. The other condition was in Stratford, where I only saw him twice, both times in springtime. And my memory of him is of his overflowing welcome of good-will and kindness. . . . Then I remember there was sunshine both times, and he was delighting in the spring, and in being in Stratford, so near to where Shakespeare knew the spring."

Of creative work there is nothing but this little sheaf of songs, *Weeping-Cross and Other Rimes*, with a touching impression of him by M. T. D. The poems are not the poems of a professional poet : they are the fugitive cries of a man who lived all his life with the work of poets, and who now and then, under the stress of emotion, fashioned verses that are more Elizabethan than Georgian, and that have a curious way of arresting the attention. Here is one—an excursion of this bookish man into the

larger and less tranquil life of the world. He calls
it " Looking Forward "—

> " ' After the war,' I hear men say,
>   ' Never a war will be.
> A League of Nations will bear sway
>   O'er earth and sky and sea.'
>
> Ah, but if e'er should dawn a day
>   By Fate's malign decree,
> When England lies the sport and prey
>   Of crazed Democracy !
>
> Better unending battle-fray
>   So English hearts be free,
> Than mutely wear to dull decay
>   In ignobility."

And here is a final impression of A. H. Bullen
contributed by M. T. D.—an impression that
stays—" I can see him now, dog at heel, leisurely
pacing the rough green ridges of the great field that
leads to Shottery, while chanting under his breath
some tag or end of song. . . ."

IX. FRANCES HODGSON BURNETT

WAS it the year 1883? I think so. It may have been 1882. At any rate it was the year when I attended my first dance and had my first literary conversation with a charming but, to me, rather formidable young partner.

We had danced together tolerably well; we had adjourned to a conservatory; we were seated under a palm; above us hung a discreetly radiant Japanese lanthorn (a novelty at that time and all the rage); I was becoming aware that my surge of small talk was ebbing, when my charming partner exclaimed suddenly, " I hated coming here to-night."

My face expressed chagrin. I was too young to be anything but frank, and she, noting my embarrassment, added quickly, " Of course I like dancing with you, but—but when the time came to dress I was deep in the most lovely story I have ever read. It is be-au-ti-ful. I shall finish it to-night before I go to sleep. I should adore to meet Bertha and Colonel Tredennis, and dear Senator Blundel."

" What is the book called? Who is it by? " I asked in my practical way; for even then I was beginning to be interested in authors.

But my fair companion was still in the " story " stage : she had not reached that state of culture when a reader is interested in the author, and realizes that there may be significance in a title.

She frowned prettily. " It's about an Administration, something that happens in American politics —and oh, the author's Christian name is Frances."

" *Through One Administration,* by Frances Hodgson Burnett," I suggested. " I read it in *Scribner's.* It's a jolly fine book."

My companion looked at me admiringly. " Yes, that was the name. *Through One Administration.* You *are* clever."

.   .   .   .   .

I have just re-read this charming story after a lapse of nearly thirty-eight years, and find its charm still persuasive. It is natural; it is full of sympathy and understanding; it accepts sentiment as a concomitant of life, which is the view of most people, in spite of the hard-headed novelists who are popular to-day; and it shows that Mrs. Burnett is a born story-teller.

Is it still read? I observe that Mr. W. L. George does not include Mrs. Burnett in his division of British novelists into the Neo-Victorian, the Edwardian, and the Neo-Georgian; but perhaps Mr. George regards Mrs. Burnett as an American. In law she is, as her first husband was Dr. Burnett of Washington.

She was born at Manchester, England; at the age of sixteen she was taken by her parents to Knoxville, Tennessee. She travels much, and it would seem that she has not quite been able to make up her mind about her nationality, as in the English *Who's Who* she gives her address as Maytham Hall, Rolvenden, Kent, and in the American *Who's*

Who as Plandome, Long Island. That, I think, is her real home. There in recent years she wrote *The Shuttle*, *T. Tembaron* and *The Head of the House of Coombe*. She likes to spend her winters in Bermuda.

Her literary activities are many and various. They include "Juveniles," as books written for children are called; and so I come to that delightful study by this most natural, most sincere, most sympathetic of writers, who has never acquired a manner because her style is herself; who has not modelled herself on anybody; whose books show not the slightest influence of Turgenev, Flaubert, de Maupassant or Meredith; who just writes on simply and directly because she has the story-teller's gift (it's a rare gift), and a rare feeling for and understanding of children. Rightly she gives her recreation as "Improving the Lot of Children."

The book whose title I skirted a few lines above is *The One I Knew the Best of All : A Memory of the Mind of a Child*. The child is, of course, Mrs. Burnett herself. We are shown not only, in the frankest and most engaging manner, the growth of the mind of a child, but also the beginnings of a natural writer, so simple, so inevitable. Young people who are in the habit of asking successful authors how to begin authorship should read the chapter called "Literature and the Doll." With this child there was no beginning, just a gliding into writing with as little effort as taking a walk, when one foot, without thought, follows the other. The young author with imagination, or even with fancy, never asks advice. He or she simply writes dreams. Whether they are marketable or not rests much with editors and publishers. Of course imagination was always present with this Child in *The One I Knew the Best of All*, and always alert.

" It was a wonderful world—so full of story and adventure and romance. One did not need trunks and railroads ; one could go to Central America, to Central Africa—to Central Anywhere—on the arm of the Nursery Sofa—on the wings of the Green Arm Chair—under the cover of the Sitting Room Table."

And at the end of the book we are told how this writing child, in her thirteenth year, had two short stories accepted and paid for. The child showed a clear head and clear understanding, exemplified in the last sentence of her letter to the editor when she submitted her first story. The line has often been quoted. It was, " My object is remuneration."

And *Little Lord Fauntleroy* ? I must have read it half a dozen times. I read it again yesterday, and the lump rose once more to the throat, and the mist once more to the eyes, and I am not ashamed to own it, for the gallant little Lord is of the stuff that makes the world a better place through a philosophy that believes always the best of people, and, lo, they become better at the first instant of believing in them. *Little Lord Fauntleroy*, in book and play, has fluttered into a myriad of hearts. So has *Editha's Burglar*, again the theme of Innocence conquering through simple art of being true and fearless.

Mrs. Burnett's first success was *That Lass o' Lowrie's*, published in 1877, a story of mining life in the north of England, crammed with dialect, a human tale, simply and sympathetically told. It bears reading again in these days of Labour troubles, for this North Country tale deals with the beginnings of the disputes between masters and men. Here is a significant passage—

" The substitution of the mechanical fan for the old furnace at the base of the shaft was one of the projects to which Derrick clung most tenaciously. During a two years' sojourn among the Belgian mines, he had studied the system earnestly. He had worked hard to introduce it, and meant to work still harder. But the miners were bitterly opposed to anything ' new-fangled ' and the owners were careless."

Many, many other books, short stories, and Juvenile tales, have come from the pen of this prolific, conscientious, sensitive and sympathetic " born writer." Had she produced nothing but *Through One Administration, Little Lord Fauntleroy* and *Editha's Burglar,* these three alone would suffice : they have endeared her to the children and to the adults of two nations.

I count myself her devoted admirer, and some day, perhaps, I shall contrast Mrs. Burnett's way of writing about children with Mr. Kenneth Grahame's.

X. JOHN BURROUGHS

"LET us have a John Burroughs picnic," I said.

"What is a John Burroughs picnic?" they cried.

"Oh, you simply bear him in mind during the picnic, talk about him at intervals, try to be conscious of his presence when you are attracted by a plant, a tree, or a bird; and each of you, when the talk languishes, should intrude with a view of Burroughs, or a memory, or a reflection. That's a John Burroughs picnic. Don't stress the note: don't let us force ourselves to be thinking of him at every twist and turn of the walk; just let him be the presiding influence—that's all."

"On New Year's Day," said Mary Ann, "my husband gave me a copy of John Burroughs' latest book—*Accepting the Universe*. I read the last essay first, I always begin at the end of a book. The essay is on Walt Whitman. He knew Walt for thirty years. The essay is a wonderful pan-e— panegr——"

"Panegyric," I suggested. "Good. Bring *Accepting the Universe* along with you. Yes, yes! We shall have time for a little reading after luncheon, and I don't mind telling you that I shall ask you to listen to a passage or so from two books on him that I have in my bag upstairs—*Our Friend John*

Burroughs by Clara Barrus, and *Rambles with John
Burroughs* by de Loach. I also have a big envelope
crammed with newspaper extracts and photographs ;
and if the post is on time I may get from New York
John Burroughs, Boy and Man, also by Clara Barrus,
his secretary."

Belinda smiled. "That's his way," she said.
"When he's going to write on an author he entices
his friends to express themselves on the subject."

"Yes," I answered, "I try to relate authors to
life, not to libraries. And you know what you have
to do on the walk, don't you, Belinda ? "

"I suppose I must make a list of the plants and
trees that I stop to look at—the kind of things
that John Burroughs might have liked to hear
about. Do you know that I was once mistaken
for him ? "

"WHAT ! ! " we all shouted.

"Yes. Some years ago I wrote the Introductory
Note to an exhibition of pastels, chiefly of flowers,
by an American artist for a London exhibition.
I signed the note J. B., Jean Brenchley, my mother's
name. The art critic of the London *Times* spoke
very highly of my effort, and he actually said that
no doubt J. B. stood for John Burroughs."

"Good for you," said Patricia.

Then we began to walk.

We had all taken the walk before (Virginia, U.S.A.,
was the place), and we all loved it : our aim is to
follow the river bank as far as the dam, a toilsome
adventure, for it is ever our purpose not to wander
farther than ten yards from the water, which means
jumping freshets, and evading undergrowth ; but

it is worth any trouble to reach the green meadow that stretches down to the dam, a Niagara in little, such colours, such a glory of tumbling iridescent water.

In the party there was Belinda, the Painter, the Painter's wife, Mary Ann, Patricia, young Mulvaney and myself.

Young Mulvaney is not literary. He prefers automobiles to books, and he would have fled from the Burroughs picnic had not Patricia been of the party. So I was rather gratified when Patricia made it quite clear that she meant to walk with me. By the by, Patricia is young, charming and intelligent, and, of course, she cannot help being Irish. When I tell her this a curious and most becoming light flashes into her eyes. Well, she walked resolutely by my side, and I was wondering how I should entertain her, when she suddenly directed my thoughts into the channel that suited her. The Irish, I am told, are like that. Said Patricia—" I know a lot about Chaucer, and somebody else whose name I have forgotten. We studied them last term. But who is John Burroughs? You might be nice and tell me before the others discover my ignorance." She took my arm and turned her head away from young Mulvaney, who was showing off in mid-stream, jumping from boulder to boulder.

" Delighted," I said, " but I warn you that I am just learning all about him myself. You heard Belinda explain my method. Ha! ha! By the by, where is Belinda? "

We spied her far up the bank digging into the old

leaves for a shy plant that she had detected.
" Belinda has found something that would have
interested John Burroughs," I remarked. " Belinda
is a nature lover. After me, nature is her cardinal
consolation."

Patricia smiled. " Begin about John Burroughs,"
she said.

" He was the patriarch or dean of American letters
and he was the most beloved figure in American
literature. Not only was he the most popular of
American naturalists, but he was also a philosopher—
not a muddle-headed philosopher, but one who
wrote the clearest style, and who convinced you, in
every paragraph, of his radiant sincerity. He did
not think with his pen in his hand as so many writers
do : he collected and marshalled his thoughts
beforehand, and he was so fair and just that whether
you agreed or disagreed with him you caught his
optimism, and you could not help having an immense
affection for this stalwart out-of-doors man, who
lived the simple life with simplicity and avidity,
never with the pose that characterizes so many simple-
lifers. You must certainly read his *Accepting the
Universe*, which may be regarded as his mature and
final statement about nature and man. And I'll
lend you my pile of cuttings of ' John Burroughs'
Notes on Nature,' three questions, and three
answers, which appeared each day last year in a
syndicate of American newspapers. I read them
every day with delight, and at dinner-parties I
astonished people by my knowledge of, and answers
to, such questions as—' Is watercress a wild plant ? '
' Are there large springs in Florida ? ' ' Do animals

think ? ' ' How do baby ducks reach the water from their nests high in the tree-tops ? ' ' "

" You are very assimilative," said Patricia, " and I am very inquisitive. Tell me something about the life of John Burroughs, what books he wrote and where he lived."

" In early life he ' taught school,' became a treasury clerk, then took up farming, and finally devoted himself to literature and fruit culture— a good combination. He wrote on Whitman, and published many nature books such as, *Wake Robin, Signs and Seasons, Bird and Bough, Camping and Tramping with Roosevelt, Leaf and Tendril.* He was a great Emersonian, and the first article he published, called ' Expression,' issued in the *Atlantic Monthly,* in 1860, unsigned, was generally ascribed to Emerson. But J. B. was a wise man. Quickly he decided, ' I must get on ground of my own. I must get this Emersonian musk out of my garments at all hazards.' That he did, and for years and years all that he wrote was pure John Burroughs—sane, clear, kindly, wise. With him the style was indeed the man. He lived on the Hudson, a few miles below Pough-keepsie. His home, his houses, his woodland retreats, there were three of them, I think, up there in the Catskills, are places of pilgrimage. You will read all about him and his visitors in the charming books I have with me by Clara Barrus and R. J. H. de Loach."

" We might have a Burroughs picnic in the Catskills," said Patricia.

Just as I was about to reply we came in sight of the green meadow. We were asked why we had dallied so. I did not explain. But the picnic was a great success. I showed them my photographs of Edison, Henry Ford, and John Burroughs at their annual reunion at Yama Farms, Napanock, New York, and of John Burroughs and Henry Ford matching their skill at tree felling. I read them picked passages from J. B., then we talked, and each contributed something to the symposium. The honours fell to Belinda and young Mulvaney.

Belinda, who had been steadily writing in her pocket-book, three pages, each side covered, read aloud the list of the plants and things she had found on the walk that " might have interested John Burroughs." I shall use this list in my essay on the naturalist. It will save me at least a page of writing.

As for young Mulvaney, he appeared when luncheon was half over, covered in mud and dripping water, and after eating much too quickly suddenly he said : " Why, I believe I know something about the man you're gassing over. Yes, I'm sure it was he. I was motoring through Toledo in 1918, and got held up outside the Art Museum—there's a kind of park there—by the largest number of children I've ever seen in my life. There were thousands of them, and they all went up, one by one, to a smiling, thin, and quick-moving man, with a straggling beard, who was standing on a terrace; and each child as he passed threw a flower at his feet, and the old fellow smiled and smiled, and by the time it was over the flowers almost reached his knees. I asked a cop what it all meant, and he said that the Mayor had decreed a Burroughs Day."

Young Mulvaney made a hit with his impromptu speech. It pleased Patricia. She walked home with him.

There was a wonderful sunset that night, with dripping wisps of feathery fire in the golden glow, so bright that it was easy to read even in the wood. Just before we parted, as a benediction to the day, I persuaded Belinda to read that poem by John Burroughs called " Waiting." It begins thus—

> " Serene, I fold my hands and wait,
>   Nor care for wind, nor tide, nor sea ;
> I rave no more 'gainst time or fate,
>   For lo ! my own shall come to me."

And ends thus—

> " The stars come nightly to the sky,
>   The tidal wave comes to the sea ;
> Nor time, nor space, nor deep, nor high,
>   Can keep my own away from me."

" I like literary picnics," said Patricia.

XI. BLISS CARMAN

WHEN I went to Canada I put into my pocket *Songs from Vagabondia*. It is full of fine things, and does not take more space than a notebook. I debated whether I should drop *Low Tide on Grand Pré* into my other pocket, for I like reading books in the places where they were written; but *Low Tide on Grand Pré* had to give place to a less useful article.

It was my purpose when I reached Quebec to make a dash for New Brunswick on the coast, and seek out Fredericton, where Bliss Carman was born, and perhaps also cast an eye over Douglas, near Fredericton, where his cousin, Charles G. D. Roberts, saw the light—another Canadian poet and author. But I did not travel beyond Quebec, so I have been reading Bliss Carman in a chair in New York.

I have seen somewhere that this Canadian poet, " six feet three in his heelless, square-toed shoes," was to be observed years ago in his bark canoe flashing down the St. John River ; and in one of his prose books, that called *The Kinship of Nature*, he writes of " the little Canadian town on the St. John "—his home-town ; but I do not associate him with Canada. He is the poet of springtime and the open road : he is one of Nature's particular children. All the world is his home-town, any forest, any river, any place where Pan cares to hide : under

F 65

any sky, so long as there is not a city near. A wise State would give such a man a hut in a wood, three acres and a cow, weekly groceries, with a motherly person to look after him. The wise State would merely give him instructions to make songs for those unfortunates who are debarred from nature eleven months of the year. There is no place for the real poet in the world of to-day : he should be given a little competence and told to make poetry.

But as States and County Councils have not yet learned how to treat a poet, and as I suppose Bliss Carman had to earn a living (the wages of a plumber are regal compared with those of a poet), he went to New York to edit *The Independent*, and later to Boston to look after *The Chap Book*. Those were episodes. He is a wanderer, a man of the wide world, his bed should be in a tree. I remember reading an article by him in a magazine giving a description of a hut in the wood he lived in, somewhere in the Catskill Mountains, near Rip Van Winkle's country. And I preserved the headlines that the editor gave to the article—thus : " A poet tells in colourful prose (I wonder what colourful prose is) of how a mountain retreat, where he found a home for many years, may be reached by the wayfaring man." I can imagine the agony of silent, retiring, unpretentious, unclubable Bliss Carman if bevies of wayfaring men, taking the editor at his word, appeared in relays tramping through the beech trees to " The Ghost House," with Bliss Carman writing lyrics on the porch, trying to hide.

I have never been to this hut in the Catskills.

I have never tracked him to any of his haunts :
when we have met it has always been in a city, and
he has always seemed alone. Nature lovers are
like that. Man is an episode. Trees, birds and
streams are their familiars. Once I stayed for a
week in a house with Bliss Carman. He never
appeared at mealtime, or in the evening ; but when
I looked out of the window in the morning I would
sometimes see him going out, and when I looked out
of the window in the evening sometimes I would see
him coming in. And once we sat next to each other
at a supper of book collectors and book buyers.
He seemed modestly happy, and interested to see
G. D. Smith, Rosenbach and John Clawson in the
flesh, but he did not come out of his shell. Silence
is his hobby. I felt that he would have been more
at home supping with Pan off acorns and wild honey.
He was mute about himself. Had he talked cheerily
or reflectively on his own sylvan, lyrical work I should
have told him how delighted we in London in the
nineties were with his three little books, *Songs of
Vagabondia*, and other volumes by him, real songs
by a singer, who must sing as others talk. And
I should have asked him about Richard Hovey.

Some of the poems that we liked in those old
days in London I could have quoted to him, so
tenacious is memory when it loves what it learns.
One of them was—

> " Now the joys of the road are chiefly these :
> A crimson touch on the hard-wood trees ;
>
> The outward eye, the quiet will,
> And the striding heart from hill to hill ;

An open hand, an easy shoe,
And a hope to make the day go through—

O leaves, O leaves, I am one with you.
Of the mould and the sun and the wind and the dew."

And I remembered—

" The marigolds are nodding :
    I wonder what they know.
Go listen very gently ;
    You may persuade them so.

Be Darwin in your patience,
    Be Chaucer in your love ;
They may relent and tell you
    What they are thinking of."

And—

" I saw the Quaker Ladies,
    Those Innocents that strew
The flooring of the forest
    With their tiny stars of blue.

I looked upon their faces,
    Companioned yet alone ;
And this foolish heart that loved them
    Grew simple as their own.

For their eyes are full of quiet,
    And their days are full of peace ;
And I will pass to-morrow
    Content to my release,

If but the Wind above me
    Say, ' Wayfellow of mine,
There be other Quaker Ladies
    Upon other slopes of pine.' "

Looking through Bliss Carman's books—there
are over a score of them—finding old friends among

his poems, making new ones, I notice how often this
wanderer recalls the home of his youth, for the
thoughts of youth are long, long thoughts.

" Oh, there the ice is breaking, the brooks are running free,
  A robin calls at twilight from a tall spruce-tree,
      And the light canoes go down
      Past portage, camp and town,
  By the rivers that make murmur in the lands along the sea."

I began to think that I would end this article
gently, with meandering quotations from more of
his poems that I love, when a friend who knew that
I was writing on Bliss Carman said, handing me a
book, " This will interest you."

It did ! Metaphorically, in a literary way it
felled me.

It was a thick book of 254 pages, and here is the
title-page—

Université de Rennes
Faculté des Lettres

———

THÈSE DE DOCTORAT

BLISS CARMAN

A STUDY IN CANADIAN POETRY

By H. D. C. LEE

Docteur de l'université de Rennes.

PRINTED BY THE HERALD PRINTING CO., LD.

Buxton

Telephone No. 77

This thesis is done extremely well. Bliss Carman
is analyzed as if he were a Blue Book, and within the
pages is a letter giving an account of the public
" soutenance " of the thesis, and telling how the

learned doctors discussed it with force and fire; and how the dean unmercifully tore one of the chapters to threads. And all this about a lyric poet who makes little songs and loves nature.

It is as if a cook had bought a few pots of spring flowers and had placed them in a cellar, opening the trap-door in the pavement above to let air and light reach them. A coal cart approaches and the man in charge, thinking that the trapdoor has been opened for him, shoots a cartload of anthracite down upon the spring flowers.

So I close the weighty Treatise, and open again the book of this light-footed poet, open it at—

> " Now the joys of the road are chiefly these :
> A crimson touch on the hard-wood trees ;
>
> The outward eye, the quiet will,
> And the striding heart from hill to hill."

XII. R. B. CUNNINGHAME-GRAHAM

" I TOO have heard the Indians striking their hands upon their mouths as they came on, swaying like centaurs on their horses and brandishing their spears. I too have shivered by camp fires, have known night marches under the southern stars, down in the grassy pampas, far below Cholechel, in Mexico, in Texas, and in Paraguay.

"Horses I have owned, especially a little Doradillo . . . but, *basta*, that way anecdotage lies."

It is Robert Bontine Cunninghame-Graham who is speaking, or rather writing, in the Preface to his *Life of Bernal Diaz del Castillo*, one of the little band of Spanish adventurers who accompanied Cortez on his conquest of Mexico.

When I had finished transcribing the above passage, I said to myself, " Why write any more ? This is Cunninghame-Graham : this is the man."

Then I thought that I would also transcribe something he wrote about a horse in one of his Footnotes—he is an adept on Footnotes and Prefaces, for he likes to comment incisively on what he has been saying romantically ; and he loves to explain himself in his Prefaces, why he writes, and why the public is what it is, and why he goes on writing, the reason of course being that he delights to write, and to lecture the public : oh, yes, he has

Views as to the way the world is behaving and
drifting, and although a Scottish Laird, half his
heart is in old Spain, and the new Spain of Cortez,
and throughout Latin America where the soft
Spanish tongue reigns, and among the Arabs, and
nomads, who distrust cities, and love the stars, and
the fresh face of dawn, and far horizons. He travels,
and writes romantic and ironical Things Seen of the
byways of life, which he finds more vitalizing than
the high-roads.

While searching for that Footnote on the horse
I chanced upon this about Spain. It is the first
essay-story in his little book called *Success*, and I
quote it without comment : you, reader, can reflect
upon it at your leisure.

" Nothing can stand against success and yet keep
fresh. Nations as well as individuals feel its vulgar-
izing power. Throughout all Europe, Spain alone
still rears its head, the unspoiled race, content in
philosophic guise to fail in all she does, and thus
preserve the individual independence of her sons."

Still searching for the Footnote about the horse
I found a Preface dated from Fez, Morocco, and
paused to read it. Toward the end is this—

" As for myself, I sit in a neglected orange garden,
in which all day the doves coo in the trees. . . . I sit
and write this Preface to my slight tales. . . ."

Is this remarkable man, this citizen of the world,
this dainty and ironic truth-seeker, and sham-derider,
this aristocrat who is so much at home with the
proletariat, who is Laird of Ardoch and Gartmore,
and who fought in Trafalgar Square for the right of
free speech, this Member of the British Parliament,

this grandee of the mob, this Socialist Don Quixote, at heart a Spanish Conquistador; this lover of modern poetry, and author of *A Brazilian Mystic*— is he beginning to be visible and tangible?

Ah, here is the Footnote about the horse—

"To-day a good horse's mouth is hardly ever seen in England, because no need of it is ever felt. Even a polo pony turns like a collier that carries weather-helm, beside a cattle horse, either in Australia or in America, amongst the Arabs or the Cossacks of the Don."

And here is another passage from a Preface. He is writing of authors and the trail their books leave—faint or firm—

"Mine, if you ask me, are to be found but in the trails I left in all the years I galloped both on the prairies and the pampas of America. Hold it not up to me for egotism, O gentle reader, for I would have you know that hardly any of the horses that I rode had shoes on them, and thus the tracks are faint."

I have often seen him on horseback, not on the pampas or the prairies—no, in the Row, during the London season. It is only the truth to say that he is the best horseman of the many who canter along the Row, and again it is but the truth to say that he is the most distinguished-looking of the cavaliers. He carries himself in life, as in his prose, with romantic and personal air. I have been told that by birth he is the remarkable combination of a Spanish Don and a Scottish Laird, but rumour-destroying *Who's Who* is silent on the Spanish Don ancestry. He is Cunninghame-Graham of Ardoch,

and he married Gabriela, daughter of Don Francisco
José de la Bolmondière. On the few occasions
when I have ridden in the Row he has been kind
enough to salute me, and to glance disapprovingly
at my steed, as I, in editorial capacity, have glanced
disapprovingly at his handwriting. He may be the
best horseman in the British Isles : he is certainly
the worst caligraphist.

Our meeting-ground has been a certain club in
St. James's Street. Thither, when in London, it
was his habit to saunter, and there we have had many
an engaging talk about literature and life, and the
unbeaten tracks of what Mr. Oliver Herford calls
This Giddy Globe. Our conversation once turned
on Arabs, and Cunninghame-Graham offered, if I
would meet him at Fez on a certain day, to conduct
me on a camping tour through the desert. I
declined because—oh, some silly reason ! How we
miss our opportunities. I might have become a
second Robert Hichens.

Cunninghame-Graham is a subjective writer.
It is life that interests him, its irony, its pathos, its
stupidity, its blunders after freedom : he sees himself picking his way courteously through the muddle,
administering praise when his buoyant heart is
touched, and flicks of the whip when he thinks they
are needed, which is often. He is fearless ; he rather
likes to bestow these flicks with the assurance of one
who thinks that he sees more than we see (perhaps
he does) and is doing us a service in wounding our
density. Nothing human is alien to his sympathy ;
he dips into, and is at home in all strata of society,
and so we find him publishing his short essay-tales

and sketches (these are essential Cunninghame-Graham) in *The Saturday Review*, which every " gentleman " reads, and in *Justice*, which no " gentleman " reads. In style he is a rambler ; he has charm, he is whimsical, but you always feel that he is writing to please himself, not the bigwigs of literature ; and he allows himself, at will, to break off in his narrative, and indulge in quaint asides, and ironical wisps of philosophy. To some readers the sprinkling of Spanish names and place names in his stories is somewhat distracting, but persevere, and you will be rewarded. In each tale he says something, reveals something, that you feel to be truth, and not the obvious truth. At heart he is a builder of a new world, while enjoying the present one, somewhat in the detached, amused, sympathetically aloof way of Lord Beaconsfield.

His essay-tales and sketches are collected in little books under such titles as *Success, Progress, Faith, Hope, Charity*, titles chosen by the author with intention, and perhaps with the idea of giving a jar to the self-satisfied.

He is also an historian, and a very fine historian, vivid—with the power of making facts picturesque. I have heard his *Hernando de Soto* described as a masterpiece, and himself placed " in the front rank of historians past and present." The *Life of Bernal Diaz del Castillo* is a spacious and glowing piece of work, and seems to show that he enjoys a large canvas after working in miniature ; and I found *A Vanished Arcadia* moving and touching : he actually made me interest myself in the history of Paraguay. Here, too, is a Preface : and here is

the beginning of it.   He loves to explain the why of
everything, including himself, and his power to
write history—

"I am aware that neither my calling nor election
in this matter are the least sure.   Certain is it that
in youth, when alone the historian or the horseman
may be formed, I did little to fit myself for writing
history.   Wandering about the countries of which
now I treat, I had almost as little object in my
travels as a Gaucho of the outside ' camps.'   I never
took a note on any subject under heaven, nor kept a
diary. . . ."

What are notes to memory ?
One thing calls for doing, clamours—" My Autobiography," by R. B. Cunninghame-Graham.

XIII. JOHN DAVIDSON

" CAME to London 1890; wrote reviews and articles until his poetry began to attract attention. . . ."

The above is a brief extract from John Davidson's biography. There is pathos in the words "came to London 1890." Here is a type of the perfervid, hard-working, ambitious Scotch youth, determined to excel, conscious of gifts, yet not knowing quite how to use them, pouring out plays, poems and romantic novels with the quickness of talk.

In those preparatory years in Scotland he earned his living teaching in various schools—pupil teacher Highland Academy, master at Perth Academy, and so on. In 1883 we find him, no doubt bored with teaching, a clerk in a thread firm in Glasgow : then, as if he could not endure the tedium of a commercial desk, returning to junior masterships in other private schools, and while all this drudgery was going on the poet in him had produced *Bruce : a Drama, Smith : a Tragedy*, and three other plays which were issued in Greenock in 1889—plays that although he seems to have found a publisher for them he must have known had little chance of ever being produced on the stage.

I knew John Davidson well after he came to London in 1890. He was not in the least like the traditional figure of a poet : he was a short, stocky man, full of ideas, very opinionated, chronically angry with the world for not taking him at his own valuation, yet a very pleasant companion, for he was sympathetic and quick of observation. He had one recreation—walking. John Davidson was at his best during a tramp over the hills, spouting his own, and other people's poetry, incessantly. He gave me two of his books. They lie before me as I write, each inscribed with my name " from David-son." They are *Fleet Street Eclogues* published in 1893, and *New Ballads* issued in 1896. These had been preceded by *Ballads and Songs*, published in 1894, which included, perhaps, the most famous of all his poems, " A Ballad of a Nun "—

> " The adventurous sun took Heaven by storm ;
>   Clouds scattered largesses of rain ;
> The sounding cities, rich and warm,
>   Smouldered and glittered in the plain."

Perhaps the quick popular success of " A Ballad of a Nun " was, in a measure, due to Owen Seaman's parody in *Punch* called " A Ballad of a Bun," at which inner literary London laughed, and which may be said to have confirmed Owen Seaman's career as a parodist.

There is no doubt that, in the nineties, John Davidson forced his way into recognition, and was regarded as one of the coming men. At the end of *Ballads and Songs* some favourable criticisms of his work are printed. Here is a specimen from the pen of Mr. Zangwill, in the *Cosmopolitan Magazine*— " John Davidson is a prodigal of every divine gift, pouring out untold treasure from his celestial cornucopia. He will turn you a metaphor as deftly as any Elizabethan dramatist, and wields as rich a vocabulary. All these glorious gifts have found vent in the most diverse artistic or inartistic shapes—novels, dramas, eclogues, ballads, Reisebilder—some written for the market, but the bulk in defiance of it. Of these products of a somewhat riotous genius, only a few have the hall-mark of perfection."

That is sane and just criticism. John Davidson was a defiant poet and author. He crossed and angered the world, or he meant to do so, and he always had a grudge against the world that it did not receive him at once, with open arms, and gladly. In his writing he lacked charm ; he lacked persuasiveness ; he wanted to storm the heights of fame by a frontal attack ; he did not realize that there is always a quieter and subtler way round.

Yet I think that many of his poems will live. There is always a small public for the splendid rhetoric of which Davidson was a master, and there is always a small public to applaud the notes of defiance that run through his preaching. But what had he to offer a hungry world ? Certainly we were not fed by the prose " Testaments " that he issued, one after another, ending I think with *The Testament of John Davidson*. They were hearty prose, full of force and fire, but the world would have gained nothing by taking John Davidson's " Testaments " to its heart. It is his poems that contain his finest work, such a poem as that called " In Romney Marsh " that sings itself—

> " As I went down to Dymchurch Wall,
>   I heard the South sing o'er the land ;
>   I saw the yellow sunlight fall
>   On knolls where Norman churches stand.

As I came up from Dymchurch Wall,
I saw above the Downs' low crest
The crimson brands of sunset fall,
Flicker and fade from out the west.

Night sank : like flakes of silver fire
The stars in one great shower came down ;
Shrill blew the wind ; and shrill the wire
Rang out from Hythe to Romney town."

All are not as good as this. He seems to have always had an impulsion to cast his thought into verse. He goes for a holiday to Hampton Court, and writes a poem of seven stanzas about it that was simply not worth doing. Here is one of the stanzas—

" Now the echoing palace fills ;
Men and women, girls and boys
Trample past the swords and frills,
Kings and Queens and trulls and toys ;
Or listening loll on window-sills
Happy amateurs of noise ! "

Once, I remember, he was so impressed by a swinging nature article in the *Pall Mall Gazette* by Harry Cust that he turned it straightway into verse and sent it to the Editor, who printed it with a laugh.

A curious kind of buoyant vanity made Davidson think that everything he wrote was of value. Much of it was, for many of the poets of that day were over gentle and reflective and John Davidson loved to burst into their pallid ranks on his poetical war-horse. Consciously, or unconsciously, he expressed himself in a short poem called " The Pioneer," which begins—

> " Why, he never can tell;
> But without a doubt,
> He knows very well
> He must trample out
> Through forest and fell
> The world about
> A way for himself,
> A way for himself."

Perhaps the most attractive of his works are the two series of *Fleet Street Eclogues*, which go with a lilt, and proclaim a joyous delight in the world of skies and moors, far away from Fleet Street; but as Andrew Lang observed, " One never met journalists like those in Mr. Davidson's Eclogues— men pining in Fleet Street for the country."

> " I would I lay beside a brook at morn,
> And watched the shepherd's clock declare the hours;
> And heard the husky whisper of the corn,
> Legions of bees in leagues of summer flowers."

Journalists do not talk like this. Perhaps they would be better and happier men if they did.

His plays I have never been able to read through. One only, *Smith : a Tragic Farce*, ever had any attraction for me. Here is the title-page of his collected dramas : " Plays by John Davidson, Being : An Unhistorical Pastoral : A Romantic Farce : Bruce, a Chronicle Play : Smith, a Tragic Farce : and Scaramouch in Naxos, a Pantomime." It may be unfair to extract merely a few lines, but I stop reading when I reach such passages as—

> " IVY.—By the light of Hecate's lamp, lamp, lamp? What rhymes with lamp? Scamp? cramp?
> GREEN.—Damp."

G

John Davidson may come into his own yet.
Certainly he is not forgotten.   It has been announced
that in one district library of Manchester the
Selected Poems of John Davidson have been issued
forty-nine times since 1911.

The *Selected Poems* contain thirty-four numbers,
and I recommend anybody who is curious about this
perfervid poet to read this volume.   My eyes fall
upon a poem which opens thus—so like John
Davidson—

> " He wrought at one great work for years ;
>   The world passed by with lofty look :
> Sometimes his eyes were dashed with tears ;
> Sometimes his lips with laughter shook."

The world passes some poets by " with lofty
look " because the world is busy with many things ;
but the world is quite ready to be interested in a
poet if he approaches her persuasively and with the
art of loving-kindness.   John Davidson never did
that.   It was not his way.

XIV. GEORGE ELIOT

ON Christmas morning, in the year 1880, I, an eager and romantic youth, paced the uplands and lanes of Hampstead composing a poem on George Eliot. I may have walked where Keats walked, but I am not a poet. It was a commonplace set of verses, and yet this prosaic poem received the honour of publication. It was news and editors are human ; it was news because on December 22, George Eliot had passed away, and I felt, or thought I felt, her departure keenly. The last stanza of the poem ran—

> " George Eliot, master, woman and friend,
>   We who hopefully work on these earthly shores,
>   Now wistfully look to the distant end,
>   And ask for a life to help us like yours."

In later years when I asked the editor why he published this unpoetical poem, the good man, who was also an honest man, replied : " It was topical, and besides, your father advertised in my paper."

The present generation can hardly realize the effect of George Eliot's books on intellectual Victorian England. In her hands the novel became a sociological and spiritual exercise. It was no longer a mere story : it was a humanitarian tract, a vehicle for the demonstration of abstract moral truth. This alone would have availed little with the general public, but she also had humour, pathos, and a power of rich and varied characterization. To be sure there were anxious discussions in heterodox, as well as orthodox, families as to the propriety of her relations with George Henry Lewes, but as time passed Victorian England let the matter drop, and contented itself with her genius.

Recently I re-read *Middlemarch*, and I arose from the reading amazed at her insight and power, her poignant sympathy, her vivid characterization, her hunger and thirst for righteousness, and I saw, the pity of it, how she waterlogged the ships of her understanding with the intellectual explorations of other people. Victorian culture depended much upon great names. There were giants about— Darwin, Huxley, Spencer, Carlyle, Newman, and the German philosophers. These beacons of knowledge which Victorian England thought were final, the genius of George Eliot explored. She reflected their light and cast it on people—real fictional people, the stuff of human nature.

That eager and romantic youth, to be candid, did not derive much pleasure from George Eliot. He was too young. (I am writing like Henry Adams.) He was more interested in adventures in life than in adventures in psychology. He read *Adam Bede* for duty, he read the works of Captain Marryat for joy. But he grew up with George Eliot. Her novels were the staple food of his serious Victorian home. Book after book came out, and each was the book of the moment, of the year— *Scenes of Clerical Life*, *Adam Bede*, *The Mill on the Floss*, *Romola*, *Felix Holt*, *Daniel Deronda*. Each

was read by the family slowly and reverently, each
was discussed ("Theophrastus Such" was voted
dull), each was part of their education, and Dorothea,
Maggie, Gwendolen, Felix Holt, Romola, Lydgate,
Dinah Morris, Mrs. Poyser, Mrs. Tulliver, Hetty
Sorrel, became members of the family circle. They
discussed these fictional people, they copied the
author's profound and searching asides into their
commonplace books, and they repeated with admiration and momentary longing the only poem of
George Eliot's that has achieved popularity, of
which the first and last lines are—

"Oh may I join the choir invisible

. . . . .

Whose music is the gladness of the world."

So, on that Christmas morning the eager and
romantic youth, nurtured on George Eliot, exalted
by the idea of her effort and aspiration, conscious
of loss, made with difficulty his poem, crying for a
life "to help us like yours." That was in 1880.

How does George Eliot stand to-day? The
librarians of America (the few I have consulted) tell
a tale of unvisited shelves save when high-school
girls need her novels for class purposes. In England
she is still read, but the sale of her novels would
make a poor show against the sale of the novels,
say, of Dorothy Richardson. Miss Richardson is
entirely interested in Dorothy; George Eliot was
interested in humanity, not in Mary Ann Evans (by
the by, she adopted the *nomme de guerre* of George
Eliot because "George was Mr. Lewes' Christian

name, and Eliot was ' a good, mouth-filling, easily pronounced word ' ").

In England, where they are always faithful to favourites, 1919, the year of her centenary, was signalized at Nuneaton by a public luncheon, a children's festival, a century costume ball, with characters from her works, and a proposal to form a George Eliot society.

Reader, if you wish to be just to this great thinker and teacher, go carefully through two or three of her novels. Then perhaps you will say what the modern young woman said, who had not read a word of George Eliot, but who was fully conversant with the Russian and French novelists. *Middlemarch* came her way. She read it with avidity, passing from a patronizing attitude to one of absorbed attention, and when she had finished it drew a long breath and cried : " Why didn't they tell me about her ? Are there any more like this ? " And run through her *Life and Letters*. You will realize with amazement her unresting intellectual activity. Here is a list of the books she was reading in August, 1868, long after she had become famous as a novelist : First book of *Lucretius*, sixth book of the *Iliad*, *Samson Agonistes*, Warton's *History of English Poetry*, Grote, second volume, *Marcus Aurelius*, *Vita Nuova*, Volume IV. chapter i. of the *Politique Positive*, Guest on *English Rhythms*, Maurice's *Lectures on Casuistry*.

Such arduous study had been her pleasure throughout her life. She might have become a mere learned woman, a bluestocking; but she had always been conscious of a vague feeling that some time or other she might write a novel. Instinctively from childhood she had been studying people. Here is the bold statement of her beginnings : " September 1856 " (she was then thirty-seven) " made a new era in my life, for it was then I began to write fiction. . . . One morning as I was thinking what should be the subject of my first story, my thoughts merged themselves into a dreamy doze, and I imagined myself writing a story of which the title was ' The Sad Fortunes of the Reverend Amos Barton.' "

Scenes of Clerical Life was immediately successful, and book followed book with increasing reputation, so that in the end this student who spoke and wrote four languages, who supplied the profounder articles for the *Westminster Review*, who translated Strauss and Spinoza, who lost her faith and consoled herself with duty, became one of the five great Victorian novelists, the other four being Dickens, Thackeray, Meredith, and Hardy. Gradually her great heart mastered her mentality, her interest in humanity dominated her interest in the intellects of others, pity and tenderness coloured the chill austerity of the student.

It is impossible to write about George Eliot without quoting the description by Frederick Myers, which once read is never forgotten—

" I remember how, at Cambridge, I walked with her once in the Fellows' Garden of Trinity, on an evening of rainy May; and she, stirred somewhat beyond her wont, and taking as her text the three words which have been used so often as the inspiring trumpet call of men—the words God, Immortality,

Duty—pronounced with terrible earnestness how inconceivable was the first, how unbelievable the second, and yet how peremptory and absolute the third.   Never, perhaps, have sterner accents affirmed the sovereignty of impersonal and unrecompensing Law.   I listened, and night fell, her grave, majestic countenance turned toward me like a sibyl's in the gloom ; it was as though she withdrew from my grasp, one by one, the two scrolls of promise and left me the third scroll only, awful with inevitable fates.   And when we stood at length and parted, amid that columnar circuit of the forest trees, beneath the last twilight of starless skies, I seemed to be gazing, like Titus at Jerusalem, on vacant seats and empty halls—on a sanctuary with no presence to hallow it, and heaven left lonely of a God."

. . . And there was light. "Why," asks a modern critic, " did she not push at her prison gates and come out ? " It is an unfair question. Hers was a great nature chilled by the creeping cold of a Time Spirit whose essential quality was Fear.

. . . And there was light—light shining and waiting for this great thinker, who washed the pan of theologies, and found in the residuum only Duty.

She sought the light in what man had written and preached. The source of the light was too simple to be seen by this thinker.

XV. ST. JOHN G. ERVINE

DRAMATISTS may be born, not made; but two modern dramatic successes were achieved by men whose natural talent was shaped or made by contact with the stage. John Drinkwater learned his technique at the Birmingham Repertory Theatre, St. John Ervine at that crèche of dramaturgy, the Abbey Theatre, Dublin.

Each is an all-round man of letters. Drinkwater specializes in poetry and essays, Ervine in novels and general articles. Each has flashed into great theatrical success, and Ervine, I am convinced, will find that the stage is the appointed vehicle of his talent.

Until the production of *John Ferguson* in New York I knew little about St. John Ervine. I liked him. I like him because he is a level-headed Irishman, who keeps cool and plays fair, a blond Belfaster, with a neat turn for writing, who has been in an insurance office in London, who has written novels and plays, who fought well in the war, and who, when his fighting days were over, slipped away to Cornwall to continue the pursuit of that pleasant, but not very profitable occupation of living by the pen.

It was when he was in Cornwall that the famous cable reached him. My facts are right. He told me them himself when he was last in New York. We dined together at the house of Miss Zoë Akins,

who had just made a great success with *Déclassée*.
I watched Ervine closely and decided that, socially,
he is, like E. V. Lucas, an observer, not an actor.
He would rather make a mental analysis of a remark,
with a subtle smile flickering on his face, than cut a
dash in conversation. He notices and reflects; he
remembers things said: he told me that he has an
extraordinary ear for dialect, and that if he were in
New York for a year he would be able to report the
East Side method of speech exactly. After reading
Mixed Marriage, I can well believe this.

To return to that cable. It was a fine day, and
the cable, figuratively, came to him from the blue:
it was from the Theatre Guild of New York, asking
permission to produce *John Ferguson*. Ervine could
hardly believe the message. He consulted Bernard
Shaw, who gave him some facetious advice which
Ervine did not take. He is level-headed. I have
since learned that the president of the Theatre
Guild had picked the volume, by chance, from the
plays shelf at Brentano's, and on reading it had
been so impressed that he had called the com-
mittee of the Theatre Guild together: hence the
cable.

I was present at the first performance of *John
Ferguson*, and was much interested in the attitude
of the audience. The play was a success from the
first five minutes. St. John Ervine is a realist in
the finer emotions and aspirations, and he has the
art to make his men and women seem natural people.
From the rise of the curtain his characters were
talking and behaving as they do to this day in the
kitchen of a farm-house in County Down. This

may not be a novelty in Dublin or London, but it
was a novelty in New York. There was something
more. When the curtain rises John Ferguson is
reading aloud from the Psalms of David—" I will
extol thee, O Lord; for thou hast lifted me up. . . .
Sing unto the Lord, O ye saints of his, and give
thanks at the remembrance of his holiness. . . .
Weeping may endure for a night, but joy cometh in
the morning."

"Them's grand words," says John Ferguson,
holding up the Bible.

The sophisticated New York first-nighters were
thrilled. They looked at one another, as if saying—
"Grand words indeed! Augustus Thomas and
George M. Cohan, at their best, never wrote
anything like this. St. John Ervine has a fine
command of language."

Yes, *John Ferguson* was a success in the first five
minutes. I saw the play twice, and in the interval
I read William Archer's excellent book on *Playmaking* and I realized how slightly books and
dramatic schools can help the would-be dramatist.
Ervine is a natural playwright, for he depends for
his effects on the thoughts and actions of his characters. Only an author with an instinct for the
theatre can tell what will " go " on the stage.
Ervine himself has said : " When I write a play, I
do not think of a theatre at all. To this day,
although I have had control of one, I am almost
completely ignorant of the technical business of the
stage. When people ask me questions about
' battens ' and ' limes ' and ' flies ' I have to ask
them what these things are. I can never remember

which is the o. p. side of the stage without doing a
sort of sum in mental arithmetic."

It is just this entire absence of theatricality that
I find so attractive in St. John Ervine's plays. He
takes a section of life, usually of people in modest
circumstances, usually his own Northern Irish,
whom he knows and understands as individuals and
in groups, as a shepherd knows his sheep. Orange-
man and Catholic, Carsonite and Sinn Feiner,
stubborn father, sensitive mother, romantic son,
they all pass before us. Why, you can learn more
about the Irish question from an Ervine play such
as *Mixed Marriage* than from all the Blue Books
and Commissions that have been inflicted upon the
world. But he is no politician. He observes.
He relates. The audience can draw the moral it
likes.

His one-act play *The Magnanimous Lover* was
received with as little favour in Dublin as Synge's
Playboy of the Western World. An Irish audience
does not like to see its romantic dream of itself
dispelled. Ervine replied in an amusing way to
the protesters against *The Magnanimous Lover*.
He wrote a little play called *The Critics* and attached
to it this note : " I desire to acknowledge my debt
to the dramatic critics of Dublin for much of the
dialogue in this play. I lifted many of the speeches,
making no alterations in them, from the criticisms
of *The Magnanimous Lover* which were printed
in Dublin newspapers on the day after its first
production."

Maybe *Jane Clegg* is even a better play than
John Ferguson ; but with me the last Ervine play

I have seen is always the best. Just now I am
enthusiastic about *Mixed Marriage*, which I saw
recently, and was so impressed and moved that I
had to go behind the scenes afterward to congratulate
one of the actors whom I knew, and through him
the rest of the company. To show how little
Ervine cares for adventitious aids I may tell you
that the scene of each of the four acts is laid in the
same kitchen of a workman's home in Belfast. The
drama unfolds—inevitably. I have to use that worn
word. The dialogue? I dreaded to lose a line.
It is as ordinary as bread-and-butter, and yet it is
art. You might hear such talk in any Irish kitchen,
but you don't. Anyhow one feels that it is absolutely
real and true to life, and—well, here again is the
Irish " question " fairly and squarely presented. I
cannot help thinking that, in past years, if those in
authority who were chosen to settle the Irish question, both sides, had sat together in the stalls studying
this play with open minds they would have seen
light.

I am such an admirer of St. John Ervine as
dramatist that I have been disinclined to consider
his work as novelist. It was unfortunate that I
should have read his latest book, *The Foolish Lovers*,
first. It did not interest me, and I read no more
Ervine novels until a friend, whose judgment I
trust, began praising *Alice and a Family*. I read
it. A delightful book of the Pett Ridge kind, with
an abrupt ending, as if the author had yawned and
said : " This has gone on long enough." *Mrs.
Martin's Man* is well constructed, but I do not find
in it the allure, and the direct vision of his plays.

Changing Winds I have not read. Ervine has said that *Changing Winds* is his biggest success, but that he likes *Mrs. Martin's Man* much better.

The author of *John Ferguson*, *Jane Clegg* and *Mixed Marriage* knows his own mind, and he is able to express it. To an interviewer he made this Straight Statement:

" No, sir, I am not a Sinn Feiner and I'm not a Carsonite. Both factions hate me. I am an Irishman, but not a hater of England. I see her errors, but also her attempts to repair them, and I won't wallow in the past for anyone."

His foot is well up the ladder of success. It's a square, fine climb he has before him, as they say in County Down.

XVI. "MICHAEL FAIRLESS"

WHEN a modern book reaches a forty-eighth edition, I, being interested in the ways of the reading public, as well as in the thoughts of authors, sit down and read or re-read it carefully to discover, if possible, the meaning of these forty-eight editions.

I had read *The Roadmender* before. I read it in 1902 when it was first published, a modest little book in a green cover, and if anyone had said to me, "Do you think it will sell a quarter of a million copies in nineteen years, and that there will be Large Paper Editions, and Editions de Luxe, illustrated, and copies on vellum, all sorts of copies cheap and costly?" I should have answered, "*The Roadmender* is a nicely written little book, showing a great faith, and a great love of nature, and nice people who love nature and who have a firm faith in the final triumph of good will like it very much. For the author is sincere. She loves God, and all living things down to the smallest gentian, and she expresses herself in poetical prose, that carries the reader along in happy companionship if he is not in a hurry, and when he has finished it he puts the book down in a glow of cheerfulness and pride, for he has been given a sight of the unconquerable spirit of the author."

All this I should have said, but if I had been asked

point blank, " Will this book sell a quarter of a million copies, and run through forty-eight editions, and show no sign, at the beginning of 1922, of having exhausted its popularity ? " I should have answered, " It's an intimate, helpful book, and if I were an idealistic publisher I might like to publish *The Roadmender*, but I should expect to lose money by it."

That just shows how wrong I should have been, and how difficult it must be to be a successful publisher.

The Roadmender was first issued in 1902 as by " Michael Fairless," and each edition has borne that name ; but it did not require any great perspicacity to discern that the author was a woman, a young woman, and that she was an invalid, incurable, and that she lived a rich inner life, and that her joy in the things that are not seen was so consistent and so buoyant that no disability ever affected her. She had a marvellous gift of looking on the bright side of everything, losing sight of the gloom because of the light that shines behind it.

For years the secret of her identity was well kept. This was intentional. Those who had charge of *The Roadmender* after " Michael Fairless " had passed away, desired that her personality should be hidden from the public gaze. The book contained her message. There was nothing else to tell.

But as edition after edition of *The Roadmender* was called for, and the name " Michael Fairless " became widely known, paragraphs began to appear in the papers guessing at her identity, and articles

were written by literary pilgrims, with Sherlock
Holmes attributes, who, with the landscape
descriptions in *The Roadmender* and certain topo-
graphical features as guides, grew warmer and
warmer, as children say in their game, in regard to
the locality of the " Michael Fairless " country.
One investigator, more successful than the others,
stated in an article full of feeling and reverence for
" Michael Fairless," that, although they know it
not, passengers in a daily motor-coach ride from
Brighton stop at a village which is in the very
neighbourhood of *The Roadmender* country.

All this is, of course, but of extraneous interest.
Those who care for literature know that a book,
like a play, is " the thing," and that is really all that
matters. I am telling the story because it shows
how deeply interested all sorts of men and women
were in *The Roadmender* and its author, even years
after the book had been published. As the guesses
continued, and as some were wrong, a little volume
about " Michael Fairless " was issued by " those who
know." But for present purposes I copy out the
" Foreword " to the forty-eighth edition, which tells
all that need be known—

" The country amid which Margaret Fairless
Barber (' Michael Fairless ') wrote *The Roadmender*
is that central part of Sussex drained by the river
Adur, perhaps the least known of the three main
rivers, Ouse, Adur and Arun, which breach the
South Downs. From Chanctonbury Ring to Ditch-
ling Beacon the Downs belong to the Adur, and this
is the country of *The Roadmender*. Here, from
under the ' stunted hawthorn,' the eye looks down

H

on the one side to the ' little church ' on the Weald,
and on the other to the more distant ' to and fro
of the sea.' Over all this Wealden valley the ' long
grey downs ' keep watch, and on the inland side a
constant companion of the roads is the spire on
' the monastery where the Bedesmen of St. Hugh
watch and pray.'

"Michael Fairless wrote Parts I. and II. of
The Roadmender in a farm-house at Mock Bridge on
the Adur near Henfield, and here . . . she lay
writing ' The White Gate,' looking out over the
' pasture bright with buttercups where the cattle
feed.' "

The book is divided into three sections : " The
Roadmender," " Out of the Shadow," " At the
White Gate." The first section gives the title to
the volume, and I remember my disappointment
that the Roadmender did not continue his com-
mentaries until the last page. The other two sections
are beautiful, full of a radiant and refreshing
philosophy, but one is so interested in the actual
Roadmender that one misses him, even though the
same optimism inspires the following chapters.
They are reminiscent rather than actual.

Of course there was no real Roadmender. The
idea is symbolic, a delicate, literary artifice. And
he is not really a Roadmender at all. He is a stonebreaker. Every pedestrian and motorist has seen
the Ancients who sit on a heap of stones by the
roadside breaking the flints with a hammer. John
L. Macadam, a Scottish engineer and inventor of the
system of macadamizing roads, laid down the rule
that every stone should be broken small enough

to pass through a finger ring, or was it a curtain ring?

There never was such a Roadmender as the spiritual imagination of " Michael Fairless " has given to us; never such a Roadmender who so loved and understood nature, and had so clear a vision of reality behind the phantasmagoria of the material world. And the book has flashes of subtle humour too; see the dialogue with a real road-mender who stopped for a gossip, and with the parson who paused to lecture and who remained to bless. The book begins—

" I have attained my ideal : I am a roadmender, some say stonebreaker. Both titles are correct, but the one is more pregnant than the other. All day I sit by the roadside on a stretch of grass under a high hedge of saplings and a tangle of traveller's joy, woodbine, sweetbriar, and late roses."

And on Sundays, her day of rest, she would lie flat on a height, gazing out from the top of the downs to the sea—

" The hours pass, the shadows lengthen, the sheep-bells clang; and I lie in my niche under the stunted hawthorn watching the to and fro of the sea, and Æolus shepherding his white sheep across the blue. I love the sea with its impenetrable fathoms, its wash and undertow, and rasp of shingle sucked anew."

It is not difficult to understand why the public has taken *The Roadmender* to its heart. For it is a book written from heart to heart. This small volume stands as a proof of the statement that everyone has one book in him or in her, if they but have the gift of expression. "Michael Fairless" had it abundantly; and it is most satisfactory to know that a book of this kind, not much reviewed in its early years, not much discussed, has found a public of 250,000 people, and more.

XVII. ANATOLE FRANCE

HAPPILY I preserved that picture I cut from the pictorial section of a newspaper last year. It is a document, this portrait group of six people standing in the open door of a country house. On the right is a nice-looking woman with a large bunch of flowers inserted in her belt. This is Madame Jacques Anatole Thibaut, better known as Madame Anatole France. He, the unique Anatole France, easily first of French men of letters, stands in the centre, tall, erect, with the big, square brow, the long curling moustache and pointed beard that he sometimes remembers to trim. But that which draws me are the watching eyes, so shrewd, so reflective. The others in the group are merely posing for their photographs. He is watching the camera, the operator, reflecting, curious, as always, about everything in life and in books, in thoughts and in deeds. Underneath this photograph is printed, " Anatole France and his bride, who was Mlle. Laprevotte. Taken on their wedding day at Bechellerie, the bridegroom's estate near Tours."

From the pad where this photograph is preserved I withdraw other documents, a medley of them. There is his letter to the French Minister of War, written at the outbreak of hostilities, in 1914, when France was in danger. This Socialist, this scholar, this great dilettante, this pacifist, offers his services

in any capacity in the field.   France is in danger.
His whims about patriotism, his hatred of violence
are forgotten.   He offers all ; but he does not forget to make his offer in exquisite phraseology, for
whatever he writes is always beautifully constructed
with the clarity and simplicity of which the French
have the secret.

Next is a page of his handwriting from his War
book (very Anatolian) called *The Path of Glory*, a
rambling, discursive calligraphy, without an erasure,
firm, but with a tendency, here and there, to a
flourish.   I read his French with interest, enjoying
his ability always to place the accents just where
they should be.   Follows an editorial (I am still
going through the pad) on his great speech to the
teachers at Tours.   " Make hate be hated," he told
them.   " Burn all those books which teach hatred.
Exalt work and love."

Here is another editorial on " The Boy Anatole,"
he who was cradled in a bookshop on the Quai
Malaquais ; who as a child " played with dumpy
duodecimos as with dolls," yearned for military glory,
then for sainthood, and at the age of ten decided
that it was finer to make catalogues in his father's
shop than to win battles.

Then I took from a shelf a battered copy of
L'Étui de Nacre (" The Box of Pearl "), that marvellous collection of short stories, containing " The
Procurator of Judea," and " The Juggler of Notre
Dame," the first work by Anatole France that I
read.   Has he, in his many books, ever expressed
himself more neatly and more fully ?   I am not a
good French scholar ; but *L'Étui de Nacre* permits

itself to be read with ease, for Anatole France has a style that is as clear as his thought. I remember, too, with great pleasure, many of the essays in his volumes called *On Life and Letters*, especially one about a performance of *Hamlet*, so charming, easy and pointed that through reading it often I knew it almost by heart. And there were two short stories that impressed me, " Crainquebille " and " Putois."

His long romances and satires I do not always succeed in assimilating. The point of view of this erudite butterfly is not always ours, and the Anglo-Saxon, reading Anatole France, while still admiring, is sometimes quite reconciled to the fact that he is not a Gaul. Much of his satirical, historical work, such as the volumes treating contemporary French history, can be followed only by a Frenchman ; but *Penguin Island*, which is considered by some the finest thing he has done, is cosmic, and those who like it revel in it.

He is not a real novelist. His romances are but vehicles for the expression of his views. When I reflect on the works by him that I have read, I find that I have forgotten plots and scenes, and recall only those parts where Anatole France himself in the person of Bonnard, Bergeret, Coignard, Brotteaux is talking. This dear, garrulous, kindly, witty, ever curious elderly gentleman who speaks through so many books, delaying the story, commenting on everything, interested in everything, is Anatole himself. He is like the carven Beau that you see in so many of Watteau's pictures : in the scene yet not of it, ever lurking in the background, smiling with sympathy, disdain, amusement and scorn, liking to be there, but always detached, a looker-on.

Anatole France is most human when he deals with his own childhood, recalling it intimately and affectionately in *The Book of My Friend*, in *Pierre Nozière*, and in *Little Pierre*.

I close my eyes and recall my bookshelves in London. I see a shelf of tall red books. I think there must be twenty-five of these handsome volumes, and others have been published since I placed the last one there. On the cover is a laurel garland, and from it hangs a medallion with a portrait of the author. Around the medallion are the words— Maître Anatole France. This is the English edition of his works issued by John Lane, a notable publishing feat, probably the only example of the publication of all the works of a living author in a translation. These volumes issued at irregular intervals came to me for review. I wrote a column about each of them, and, as I read the titles to-day, there comes back to me, bit by bit, the vast, meandering, subtle, shining world of learning, fantasy, irony, pity and scorn that is Anatole France, who wrote *The Book of My Friend*, and also that amazing, erudite, fearless *Life of Joan of Arc* that offended the many, and delighted the few.

I saw him once, heard him talk, and grasped his hand. His grasp was firm in spite of the hundreds of hands that he held that evening, smiling all the time. It was a few months before the war, in London, whither he had been inveigled by the promise of a series of ovations from his many admirers. They culminated in a banquet, followed by a reception. To anybody else it might have been embarrassing, as Anatole France does not add English to his accomplishments. But he looked quite happy through the long festivities; the shrewd, reflective, amused smile never left his face. He seemed pleased, but not exhilarated, equal to the occasion, but not overwhelmed by it. Rodin had a similar look when he was entertained in London; that night when the art students unloosed the great sculptor's horses and drew his carriage to the banqueting hall where he sat listening to the speeches in uneasy French in his honour, and smiling. The French are a polite nation.

Of the vast number of essays and books also, that have been written on Anatole France, three stand out. They are the small volume by W. L. George, the still smaller volume by George Brandes and the chapter on Anatole France by Frank Harris in *Contemporary Portraits.*

The little book on Anatole France by W. L. George is the best piece of critical work that he has done. Educated in France, familiar with French thought and French literature, he has special advantages for such a study. He analyzes the great Frenchman with candour: he praises, he is also critical. Mr. George is not an optimist. Here is his idea of an entry in the Cyclopædia of Literature of the year 3000—

France (Anatole). Pen-name of Jacques Anatole Thibaut. French writer, *b.* 1844, *d.* —. Satirist and critic. Some of his work has merit as reflecting the faintly enlightened views of an observer living in barbarous times.

Mr. Frank Harris' chapter takes the form of an interview. He did not find the satirist in a smiling mood; but he put direct questions, and received direct answers. M. France allowed his interviewer to understand that he had outgrown primitive pictures, old oak furniture, Corot, and politicians. "To me," said the master, "writing is horribly difficult—horribly;" but he acknowledged that some of his books were easier to write than the others. "But doesn't the mere power of expression grow with use and become easier?" "Not to me," replied the master; "it all depends on the ideas."

That night in the children's room of a public library the real Anatole France, so I like to think, drew near to me. On a shelf I saw an open book illustrated by Boutet de Monvel. I turned to the title-page. It was *Girls and Boys: Scenes from the Country and the Town*, by Anatole France. And on one of the pages, beneath a charming picture of a little student, was this—

> "He worked with patience and love,
> Which are the two sides of genius."

XVIII. SIR JAMES GEORGE FRAZER

THE Golden Bough by Sir James George Frazer is a classic. Writing of it *The Times* said : "The book is a great book, in just the sense in which the work of Darwin, Zola, or Balzac is great. It has explored and mapped out a new world." *The Nation* said : "It is probably the most illuminating and the most durable classic that has been produced in our language in this generation."

Have I read it through from title-page to colophon ? have I mastered the twelve fat volumes of the third edition of *The Golden Bough*, published in 1911 ? The answer is in the negative. I am candid.

But all my life I seem to have been dipping into *The Golden Bough*, reading a chapter or a passage here and there, admiring the author's sense of style, and easy organization of facts, lore and legends. And I have looked on Lake Nemi, and on Turner's picture (now in Dublin) which was formerly called "Lake Avernus : the Fates and the Golden Bough " ; and years ago when I was writing a book on Turner I copied out the opening of Chapter I. of Frazer's magnum opus. It runs : "Who does not know Turner's picture of the Golden Bough? The scene, suffused with the golden glow of imagination in which the . . . mind of Turner steeped and transfigured even the fairest natural landscape, is a dream-like vision of the little lake of Nemi, ' Diana's

Mirror,' as it was called by the ancients. No one who has seen that calm water, lapped in a green hollow of the Alban hills, can ever forget it."

Once I was standing before Turner's Golden Bough with a young literary man, who has since become famous. He said (I have given his thoughts sequence, and some grammatical accuracy) : " What a jolly book Frazer's *Golden Bough* is ! I suppose it's the greatest accumulation, beautifully told, of early modes of thought, legends and notions about religion that has ever been put together. And to think that it all started from Frazer's desire to know the meaning of a strange and recurring event that happened ages ago on the banks of Lake Nemi, why it happened, and when it first began to happen. Curious how Turner and Frazer have thus come together. But Turner wouldn't have cared two-pence about the anthropological lore of the district. Listen. This is what the National Gallery catalogue says in its note on Turner's picture : ' The Golden Bough was a branch of the tree of Proserpine, which when plucked by mortals, by favour of the Fates, enabled them to visit and return from those regions with impunity.' "

My friend continued—I can almost hear him talking—" Little did Turner think that an engraving of his picture would form the frontispiece of Frazer's *Golden Bough*. I'm glad. It gives the book unity. No, I haven't read *The Golden Bough* all through. I dip into it sometimes."

The first edition, in two volumes, was published in 1890 ; the second edition, three volumes, in 1900 ; the third, twelve volumes, in 1911. Frazer is an indefatigable student. In 1918 he published, in three volumes, *Folk-Lore in the Old Testament : Studies in Comparative Religion, Legend and Law,* his aim being to illustrate and explain certain traditions, beliefs, and customs of the ancient Hebrews by comparison with those of other peoples. During the past week I have been dipping into this with interest and a kind of sad profit. On the author's other learned books I am still less of an authority—say, *Pausanias' Description of Greece* and *Totemism and Exogamy ;* but *The Magical Origin of Kings,* parts of which have been incorporated in *The Golden Bough,* held me through a long, light summer evening.

On every page of his books it is plain that Sir James Frazer (he was knighted in 1914 for his services to literature) is much more than a student and a collector of lore and legends : he is a man of letters of fastidious classical taste. Did he not publish, as long ago as 1895, *Passages of the Bible Chosen for their Literary Beauty and Interest* ? And I remember the *Letters of William Cowper,* chosen and edited with Memoir and Notes ; and *Sir Roger de Coverley, and Other Literary Pieces ;* and *Essays of Joseph Addison, Chosen and Edited with a Preface and a few Notes.* The author of *The Golden Bough* does not control a wide torrent of literature, but what he is interested in runs deep.

Joseph Addison !

It was Joseph Addison, that accomplished, placid man, and reposeful essayist, who guided me to a better acquaintance with Sir James George Frazer than I could ever have gained from glancing with

meditative interest at his rooms in Brick Court of the
Middle Temple. Curiously it was another great,
and later, literary man who was the unconscious
means of first introducing me to the author of
The Golden Bough. Sir James Frazer sat opposite
me at the dinner given in London to Anatole France,
and I remember remarking to my neighbour : " I
have an immense capacity for social chatter. The
author of *The Golden Bough* has none."

Well, I was reading Mr. Edmund Gosse's *Books on
the Table*, and came, in time, willingly to the essay
on Sir James Frazer's three stately volumes on *Folk-
Lore in the Old Testament*, and to this passage about
" the most eminent of British and probably of
European anthropologists." It was to the point :
it placed our author. The passage runs, " To us
people of letters, he is singularly endeared by his
sedulous cultivation of style, in which Addison is
patently his master."

In the following week a piece of good fortune
befell me. I call it good fortune when the chances
of literary life bring me into personal contact with
an author whose works have been engaging my
leisure, even fugitively. Among the announcements
of afternoon lectures at the Royal Institution of
Great Britain in Albemarle Street, I read this—

" SIR JAMES FRAZER.—On London Life in the
Time of Addison."

I have always found entertainment as well as
instruction at the lectures of the Royal Institution.
A considerable number of men attend, as well as
women, which is rather rare in the lecture world.

The men, with a few exceptions, are a particular type. They have large heads, dome-shaped foreheads, and tangled, untrimmed beards. I believe them to be Victorian survivals, who acquired the lecture habit in their youth, and have never been able to break themselves of it. Whatever the lecture may be they always seem to attend. I presume they have retired from active work, have their afternoons free, and are accustomed to the rather somnolent atmosphere of the lecture theatre, finding it a reposeful change from the busy life of the streets.

There we sat; I, high up, in a secluded corner, from which I could obtain a good view of the audience as well as of the lecturer. Below me was the historic desk from which so many important lectures have been delivered. A shaded light throws its beams on the lecturer, and on his notes.

The clock pointed to one minute before three. We waited. I imagine that most of the ladies had really come to see the author of " that stupendous piece of erudition and fair reasoning, *The Golden Bough*," for I cannot believe that the sex is wildly interested in London Life in the Time of Addison. The clock pointed to three. Promptly the small door in the wall of the lecture theatre opened, and a man, a small man, with a small beard and glasses, ran, it was hardly a walk, as if he were a human rabbit, straight to the desk, and at once turned out the light. That, I think, was a characteristic action of this scholar. He does not like publicity—even from a lamp. At once he opened his manuscript and began to read, in a firm, crisp voice, which could be heard all over the theatre, and in a broad Scottish

accent.   I liked that, and I liked his impersonal way,
without an aside, without any attempt to make a
contact with his audience ; but this method of
lecturing does not make for popularity.   That,
probably, is the last thing Sir James Frazer wants.
He read straight on, clearly, forcibly, and I must confess that I was more interested in his manner than in
his matter.   He did not throw any illumination on
Addison : he did not lure that aloof figure from his
distinguished literary retreat.   Many of the Victorians nodded, but I kept wide awake.

When the lecture was over I joined the small
throng of congratulators.   When my turn came I
reminded the author of *The Golden Bough* that we
had met at the Anatole France dinner.   He had no
recollection of the occasion.   Then I complimented
him on his marked Scottish accent.   That seemed
to please him : he whispered that he was a Glasgow
man.   There our conversation ended, and I made
way for another disciple.

XIX. HAROLD FREDERIC

I MET this burly, sensitive American author on two occasions.

The first time was in the studio of a popular portrait painter, J. J. Shannon (now Sir James Shannon, R.A.), on Show Sunday, that is, the day on which pictures destined for the Royal Academy exhibition are exposed to friends and critics. In those times, the early nineties, Show Sunday was a very popular social function. The pictures were arranged attractively on easels, the visitors came and went, and tried to say something complimentary or clever. I always found that the best way was to creep quietly up to the painter, feel for his hand, and silently grasp it, firmly and warmly.

This occasion was especially interesting, as J. J. Shannon was born in America, and there was a sprinkling of Americans at this Show Sunday. The time passed so pleasantly, that when I furtively looked at my watch, and saw that it was nearly seven o'clock, I hastened to my hostess to bid her adieu, and to thank her for the delightful and unique entertainment. She bent toward me and whispered, " A few friends are remaining to supper. Won't you stay ? "

That was a wonderful evening, not only because most of the guests were eminent people, but because the talk was exceptionally good. Opposite me was a big, loosely-built man, who talked extremely well, who seemed acquainted with everything and everybody, and who had dozens of new stories. I was so much interested in him that I turned to my neighbour and said, " Do you know the man opposite ? " He replied, " Oh yes. That's Harold Frederic, London representative of *The New York Times*, but his real game is novel writing. You should read his *Seth's Brother's Wife*, and *In the Valley*."

I looked at the big man with more interest, engaged him in conversation, assuming my most modest manner, until his eyes twinkled, and he " got back " on me. Our pleasant parry and ripost was interrupted by cries for a song from Harold Frederic. He moved to the piano, with his table napkin dangling from his waist—he was rather an untidy man— and sang a series of American college songs roisterously, boisterously, yet, when the occasion demanded it, with feeling and emotion. The Americans present joined in the chorus, and the English folk emitted harmonious sounds.

" What college was he ? " I said to my neighbour.

" None," he replied. " Frederic was born in Utica, New York, went to the public schools and then became a reporter on the local paper. He was editor of *The Utica Observer* when he was twenty-four. It's like Harold Frederic to know the college songs. He's an adept at universal information. Why, he knows these songs better than most college boys."

Next week an article by Harold Frederic appeared in Henley's *National Observer*, giving a humorous and appreciative account of the evening. No names

were mentioned in this delightful article. It
astonished me, and taught me that the " live writer "
gets his material, not from the British Museum
Library, but from the happenings of each day—
a lesson that I have never forgotten.

A year or so later I met him again. It was at the
house of the gifted poet, a charming woman, and a
remarkable hostess, who wrote under the name of
" Graham R. Tomson." I was paying a dinner call.
When I entered the room Harold Frederic was
seated at the piano singing folk songs and Negro
spirituals. He was having refreshments at the same
time : the cup was on the candle stand, and a piece
of bread-and-butter and a piece of cake were on his
knee. The crumbs of each decorated his waistcoat.
Yes, he was rather an untidy man, but he sang the
Negro spirituals with true darky feeling, and I
remember that a song about Clementine was encored
three times.

Many years passed. To be explicit, it was last
week when Harold Frederic again crossed my path.
This time it was one of his books, not himself. In
those intervening years I had read most of his novels,
including his remarkable story *Illumination*, called in
the United States, for some reason, *The Damnation of
Theron Ware*, and also his witty and sympathetic
little book called *March Hares*. And I had heard
The New Exodus : Israel in Russia, very highly
spoken of. Well, last week I entered a stationery
shop in a small market town in Kent, attracted
thither, not by the picture postcards, or by the
packets of writing-paper and envelopes, absurdly
cheap, or by a Toby Jug representing John Wesley

in the pulpit, but because my roving eye had detected against one wall of the shop a range of bookshelves. Libraries of this nature, in small English market towns, are always of one kind: they are novels that have gone out of date and out of fashion, with a sprinkling of once popular belles-lettres books which are all bought by the gross. Roaming the shelves I found a copy of *Gloria Mundi*, by Harold Frederic. I was allowed to take it away and keep it a fortnight for twopence.

I read it through with interest. It is a fine book but not a great book. For the purpose of writing it, Harold Frederic " got up " English aristocratic life. The hero is a duke, but the book is much more than a mere novel of life in high society. It deals with Socialism, and an attempt to formulate a system of communal living, in which one can detect the beginning of many political actualities of the present day. The characters are well defined, some of the younger men are especially good, and the whole story has an interest that raises it above the category of mere yarns.

At the beginning of *Gloria Mundi* there are two pages of extracts from reviews of his *Illumination*. That, as I have said, was a remarkable work, but I am rather appalled by the extravagance of some of the leading English journals in criticizing it. If Harold Frederic was as exceptional a writer as some of these journals make him, how is it that his books to-day have almost passed out of circulation? *The Athenæum* called *In the Valley* "a perfect specimen of an American historical novel." *The Daily Chronicle* remarked, " Mr. Harold Frederic is winning his way by sure steps to the foremost ranks of writers of fiction." *The Review of Reviews* said : " You will place the book with your Hardys and Merediths."

No, I shall not place *Illumination* beside my Hardys and Merediths. They are in a different class, a much higher class. One has only to read a page of Hardy, a page of Meredith, and a page of Harold Frederic, to be certain of this. Like Richard Harding Davis, he was a man of the world rather than a man of letters. The profound loneliness and cloistral mental activity of Hardy and Meredith were not for him. Like so many men who have been trained in journalism, and who have sight rather than insight, he could write well on almost any subject that he chose, but your really great writer writes not because he chooses a subject, but because the subject chooses and dominates him. Harold Frederic had great talent. Hardy and Meredith have genius. There's the difference. But, oh, the difference!

XX. W. L. GEORGE

WHY does an author become popular? Why should W. L. George, whose first book, *A Bed of Roses*, was published but eleven years ago, have had so good a " press " in America? Why should he have been interviewed at greater length than other Englishmen who visit the United States, and talk about the Manhattan sky-line, the elevators, the sky-scrapers, and their own books? I am interested in these questions, because W. L. George is by way of being a new reputation to me.

When I came to America in 1917, I had not read any of his books, and I had only, so far as I knew, seen him once. That was at an annual meeting of the Authors Society in London. He made a fighting speech, and I said to myself—" Good! He treats literature seriously."

There are so many American authors to consider that I had almost forgotten about W. L. George, when, at a dinner given by the Drama League to John Drinkwater, a young woman, who told me she came from Missouri, began to ply me with questions about W. L. George. I informed her that I was old-fashioned, that he was a new man, and that I had no information about him: after a pause I said, " Why are you so interested in him? " She answered, " Oh, he is a feminist, and takes women seriously." But I found that she was only familiar with his novels. She had not read *Woman and To-morrow*, or *The Intelligence of Woman*.

He chose for the subject of his first lecture in New York, " Love and Marriage." He dined with me at a club a few days before the lecture and I begged him to change the subject of his address, on the grounds that no one wanted to hear a man talk on " Love and Marriage." He disagreed, and said, " What subject do you suggest that I should lecture upon ? " I answered, " As you have been here for three weeks why not ' What I Think of America ' ? " " Is not that a rather dangerous topic ? " he asked. " Americans, I am told, are very sensitive." " Maybe," I replied, " but you can say anything you like if only you will say it humorously, and wrap up your comment in a joke. Then you can be as caustic and critical as you desire."

He did not change the subject of his lecture. It was a crowded and attentive audience ; they followed his thought and took every point ; and, at the conclusion, the chairman (the editor of *Vanity Fair*) announced that Mr. George would be happy to answer questions. Then from all over the hall and balcony inquirers bobbed up, and many of the questions dealt with points in his novels ; chiefly the dispositions and actions of his heroines. When the lecture was over I hastened to the reception room to retract all I had said about " Love and Marriage " not being an attractive topic. " You were right, and I was wrong." He took my apology comfortably. Like Arnold Bennett he does not argue : like him he waits sanguinely until his opponent adopts his point of view.

No one at the lecture had anything to say about his thick volume called *Engines of Social Progress*, which deals with such subjects as " Small Holdings," " Housing Schemes " and " Co-operation " ; no one mentioned *France in the Twentieth Century*, with its chapters on " The French Woman " and " Marriage " ; no one asked questions relating to his valuable volume on the model town built at Port Sunlight by the proprietor of " Sunlight Soap " ; no one had a word to say on his study of Anatole France, which, in my opinion, is one of his best pieces of work. It is by his novels that he has caught the lecture public and the reading public, and I have no doubt that this is precisely what he meant to do. Here again is a similarity between W. L. George and Arnold Bennett. Neither leaves anything to chance, or to the inspiration of the moment. Each makes a literary plan of campaign, and keeps to it ; each regards literature rather as a business ; certainly as a means toward ripe living and advancement.

In my analysis W. L. George is not primarily a novelist. He is a student of sociology, a garnerer of facts, an examiner of data, and I do not believe that, in his heart, he is more interested in the condition of women than in the condition of prisoners. When I last met him he had spent the afternoon talking with the prisoners in Sing Sing, and, of all the conversational hares I started, the condition of prisoners in American jails was the one that he followed with the most eagerness. His is a practical mind, that likes dealing with and probing actualities. To a reporter, on the day after he had reached

New York, he said, " I am not one of those people
who are interested in old ruins, and Rembrandts and
cathedrals, I am interested in machinery and concrete ways of doing things, and vital things in
life. I don't care at all to visit the Metropolitan
Museum here, but I should like to visit your
law-courts."

People have different views as to what are the
" vital things in life " ; but Mr. George has no doubt
about what he thinks they are. I imagine that he
would be much more interested in the method of
carrying on a successful five-cent store, than in the
provenance of the most adorably doubtful Primitive
picture ever painted. He would be very impatient
and snappy if he were obliged to argue at length with
Ford Madox Hueffer as to the proper preparation
for writing a Great Book ; but he would be delighted
to balance with an architect the claims of a single-
material house against a two-material house at Port
Sunlight. This being so, do you not think it clever
of him to have devoted so much thought to fiction ?
for people will read a novel when they will not read a
sociological book ; and when a man wants to make
use of his knowledge it is more advantageous to
employ it in *The Second Blooming* than in *Labour and
Housing ;* and in *Caliban* and *The Strangers' Wedding*
than in *Dramatic Actualities* and *Literary Chapters*.
In the last-named book he studies and considers the
drama and literature with the same unimpassioned
detachment with which he studies love, marriage,
the French temperament and cheap cottages. His
writings lack charm. I think that he is not interested
in charm.

In *The Little Beloved*, called in the United Kingdom *The Making of an Englishman* (why do some authors have two titles for their books, one for England, the other for America ?), he depicts the process whereby " a typical French youth, mercurial, passionate, spectacular, is transformed into a staid and stolid English householder and husband." That, without the adjectives, for they describe the character in the book, is his case. He was born in France, he was educated there, he attended a French university, and it was only after being shaped into a Frenchman that he became, by choice, an Englishman. His knowledge of France and Frenchmen explains why his little book on Anatole France is so good, and perhaps that is the reason why he is quite as much interested in women as in housing.

He has written part of his autobiography succinctly in *Who's Who*. Really, I must quote it : " Educated successively as an analytical chemist, an engineer, a barrister, a soldier, and a business man ; having proved a failure at all these trades, took to journalism about 1907."

His latest novel is *Ursula Trent*. The one before was *Caliban*, a study of a " Superman " in journalism. I was immensely interested in the opening chapters, describing the school days and home life of the " Superboy," very well observed, and analyzed with energy and sound common sense ; but when the " Superman " begins to operate, the author's grasp relaxes, my interest waned, and I felt that Mr. George has not diagnosed the " Superman " with the industry and intensity with which he has analyzed the French temperament and woman.

Yesterday I sat down to make a further study of his book on *The Intelligence of Woman* (I love to learn things), but as I was beginning to master the chapter on " Feminist Intentions," someone in the next room began singing "Phyllis Is My Only Joy," and I forgot all about the book.

XXI. SIR PHILIP GIBBS

SIR PHILIP GIBBS is one of the few people whom the war has blessed. Spiritually and physically he suffered; but as a man and as a writer he has gained enormously from the part he played in the conflict. His utterances have weight. When he was lecturing in Washington an American of eminence said to me, "Hs is now a Voice."

What were his assets? Why among the multitude of correspondents did his work stand out? Why, in America and England, did people welcome his articles, read them, discuss them and regard the special correspondence of this Englishman as something separate and apart from the other columns cabled from the seat of war? His style is not vivid nor dramatic; he was given no special advantages; he did not indulge in limelight "scoops" or "stories"; by temperament and physique he was most unsuited to the ardours of the campaign. Why, then, did his war articles, books and lectures have so great a success with the English-speaking peoples? Because the heart of the people is right. Because the people saw in him a man who felt, and who had sympathy for all mankind; who told the truth; who suffered and sorrowed; but who never allowed what he saw, heard and reported to obscure his inner vision that somehow, in the end, the right would come right, and the smooth would emerge from the

rough. Such a passage as the following, taken
from his book, *The Battles of the Somme*, endeared
him to his readers. " I was only a looker-on and
reporter of other men's courage and sacrifice—a
miserable game, rather wearing to the nerves and
spirit."

He and I have met many times. Two of the
encounters stand out : an interval of ten years
between them. In those ten years he has made
good, has reached the top of his profession—descrip-
tive reporting—the most enjoyable method, in my
opinion, of earning a living, and spending one's
days. That is, if you are given a free hand, and are
not edited.

Our first meeting was in Westminster, in 1911,
in a queer, delightful twin house in the purlieus of
the Abbey, and under the shadow of the Mother of
Parliaments. There I lived, and there one day a card
was brought to me bearing the inscription, " Philip
Gibbs, Daily Chronicle." He had called to interview me on the subject of Rembrandt apropos of a
very important exhibition of Rembrandts that was
being held at Amsterdam. I have forgotten what
questions Philip Gibbs addressed to me ; I have
forgotten what I said to him. It does not matter,
because there is only one thing ever to be said about
Rembrandt—that in insight, intensity, and spiritual
communication he is the greatest artist of the world.
But I have not forgotten the look of Philip Gibbs
that day in 1911. Slight, short, pale, modest, I see
him now, standing against the window, not taking
notes, quiet, self-controlled, intent on the business
in hand, watchful, anxiously eager to draw from the

interview all he could of interest and information for the paper he represented.

He was also standing the last time I saw him in America; but the environment was very different. I saw him from the top balcony of Carnegie Hall, standing alone in the middle of the platform, his face the colour of his shirt-front, heard him speak fairly and temperately on the Irish question, heard him meet the verbal assaults of the Sinn Feiners with the composure and mild, mystical remonstrance with which he met the German bullets. And I was a witness of his triumph, perhaps the crowning success, so far, of his career. Unmoved by the interruptions, sad, not angry at their violence, as he approached the end of his lecture, he said (it was almost an aside), " I believe the great majority of Americans are friendly to the British." He was about to continue, but he paused for the simple reason that the audience broke into cheers : he did not continue because the cheers changed into shouts : he was still silent because the vast audience had risen, and was hurrahing and waving hands and handkerchiefs. Unmoved was Philip Gibbs, that is, he showed no emotion ; but his mind was working quickly, and I fancy he determined, instantly, to cut out his prepared peroration. When the cheering ceased he said simply, " You have given your answer. Thank you."

It was most effective. Indeed, I think that I have never heard a more dramatic and forcible ending to a speech. Philip Gibbs, who looks so gentle, has courage and the instinct that is given to the pure of heart to do the right thing at the right moment.

We met many times between those two episodes.
Gradually he became a figure in " the Street of
Adventure " which is Fleet Street. He had worked
his way up the journalistic ladder; had written
novels; works of history; had been literary editor
of great daily newspapers; had turned his hand to
all sorts of literary activities. So the time passed
pleasantly till 1912, when the Balkan war broke out,
and he was appointed by the *Daily Chronicle* war
correspondent with the Bulgarian armies. H. W.
Nevinson was there : he looked Gibbs over and
wondered : he beheld " the sort of dreamy youth
who would always leave his kit behind, and never
know how to get himself a square meal." With a
laugh Nevinson has since confessed how entirely he
was mistaken. The " dreamy youth " was always
alert, ready, quick, and with an amazing intuition, as
when, a few years later, he alone saw through the
humbug of Cook, the " Arctic explorer."

Philip Gibbs did well in the Balkan trouble, so
well that when the Great War broke out in 1914 his
paper, the *Daily Chronicle*, at once sent him over
to France. It was said of him, I believe I said it,
that he slipped across to France in his Fleet Street
blue serge suit with a handbag and his walking-
stick. He told me with a smile that this was near
the truth, although not quite accurate. Now and
again during those awful years he appeared for brief
intervals in his old Fleet Street haunts, always quiet,
always with more in his head than he cared to
express, always preparing to start forth again into
the confusion, folly and fatuity of war.

I read his novel, *The Street of Adventure*, a few

years ago. It has been called "a true picture of
Fleet Street" and contains, under assumed names,
the history of *The Tribune* newspaper. His novels
are bright and interesting, but I think that fiction is
not his *métier*. Nor do I think that such a clever
book as *People of Destiny : Americans as I Saw Them
at Home and Abroad* fully expresses him. The book
by him that will live is *Now It Can Be Told*, a classic,
in which he resumes and retells all he thought, and
saw, and felt in the Great War.

A man of character, he resigned the dazzling position he had reached on the *Daily Chronicle* because
he could not agree with the Irish policy of that
journal.

His pen will always be on the side of right and
justice. There is work ahead for Philip Gibbs.
He will be equal to it and—something more. That
is his way. He looks forward. One of his recent
articles is called "The Social Revolution in English
Life." Here is a sentence. "Though I see the
gravity of all this and its darkness, I believe that
England will pull through and carry on. There is
in English character still an intuitive, inarticulate
wisdom."

XXII. GEORGE GISSING

IN 1912, a book called *The Private Life of Henry Maitland*, by Morley Roberts, was published. This volume was sent to me for review by the literary editor of the London *Daily Chronicle*. " I want a signed column and a quarter," he wrote, " for a ' Published To-day ' notice. You will know how to treat it."

That was all very well : he knew that I should be in considerable doubt as to how to treat it, and he also knew that if the review were indiscreet, the blame would fall upon the reviewer. Well, I am not the first good man who has had to put up a struggle against adversity. I accepted the responsibility, read the book, reflected, and decided to tell the truth. That was an excellent idea, and it worked well. Nobody was hurt ; nobody was upset ; and I only smiled when literary friends chided me for telling the truth. I smiled because they seemed to regard the truth as something untoward and odd.

George Gissing, the only person who might have been hurt by this scrap of truth telling, was beyond praise, blame, or discoveries : he had passed away at St. Jean de Luz on December 28, 1903 : his literary reputation is secure : Frederick Harrison, H. G. Wells, Thomas Seccombe, Frank Swinnerton have written enthusiastically on him ; his secret is now known.   And at least one of his books, *By the Ionian Sea*, is regarded as a classic.

Be patient, reader.   I dwell upon this secret because the consciousness of it darkened Gissing's days, made him into a lonely, brooding man, and perhaps explains his elusive desire, shown so plainly in *By the Ionian Sea*, to escape from the present and lose himself in a scholarly appreciation of the past. His secret was, that at school he had stolen small sums of money, books and coats from his fellow-students, not for any personal indulgence, but to supply the financial claims made upon him through an action—kindly philanthropic, quixotic even—in which he allowed himself to be involved.

This sad story was known in literary circles, and to his friends, who were quite aware that most of Gissing's troubles in life were due to this compassionate, amatory strain in him.   He found it so easy to entangle himself, and so hard to untie, or even loosen the knots.   His biographers usually glide over this secret of his youth, and so are unable to give a clue to the life of this recluse, who, even when one met him in the haunts of writers, always seemed to be hovering on the outskirts of companionship.

In 1912 his old friend, Morley Roberts, who had been at school with Gissing, and who knew the whole story of his trouble from the inside, came upon the scene with *The Private Life of Henry Mait-land*, which all of us who were acquainted with Gissing and with Roberts knew, with disguised names and places, was the straightforward story of the Private and Public Life of George Gissing.   There was no doubt about it.   Every literary journalist

was aware of the story. Morley Roberts made no
secret of the enterprise, and had this not been so I
could check up incidents in the book with incidents
in Gissing's life. I even knew the real name of the
school. It was Owen's College, Manchester, and a
friend who had been a student there with Gissing
and Roberts had, long before, told me the whole
direly trivial tale. And I knew, too, that Gissing
had been diverted by his friends to America, and
that he had made good in New York, Boston, and
Chicago.

So when *The Private Life of Henry Maitland* came
to me for review I had to make a decision. I decided
to tell the truth. " Henry Maitland is George
Gissing," I said, explained how and why, and the
literary editor of the *Daily Chronicle* was so pleased
that he sent me other difficult books to review and
repeated his pleasant phrase—" You will know how
to treat them."

That was in 1912.

It was curious to read not long ago in the
" Literary Queries " column of a New York daily
newspaper this appeal—" Can any reader help me
to find out what stories were contributed to *The
Chicago Tribune* by George Gissing while he was on
the staff of that paper ? " On reading this I referred
to *The Private Life of Henry Maitland* to find Morley
Roberts saying, " I think it would be very interesting if some American student of Maitland would
turn over the files of *The Chicago Tribune* in the
years 1878 and 1879 and disinter the work he did
there."

Morley Roberts also says : " To me it seems that

he [Maitland] should never have written fiction at all, although he did it so admirably." I entirely agree with Roberts. I have read most, if not all, of Gissing's novels, and I shall never read another. They are too grey, too depressing. They have no consciousness of the Stars and the Open Gate. Even *Veranilda*, a story of Roman and Goth, which Frederick Harrison considers the " best and most original work of this really brilliant scholar," bores me. You find the real Gissing, I think, in the beginning of *Sleeping Fires*—

" The rain was over. As he sat reading, Langley saw the page illumined with a flood of sunshine, which warmed his face and hand. For a few minutes he read on, then closed his Aristophanes with a laugh—faint echo of the laughter of 2000 years ago."

And you find the real Gissing, too, in his second best book, *The Private Papers of Henry Ryecroft*, say in this passage—

" I read much less than I used to do; I think much more. Yet what is the use of thought which can no longer serve to direct life ? Better, perhaps, to read and read incessantly, losing one's futile self in the activity of other minds."

Here is another cry from " Henry Ryecroft," who is, of course, George Gissing.

" I had in me the making of a scholar. With leisure and tranquillity of mind, I should have amassed learning. Within the walls of a college, I should have lived so happily, so harmlessly, my imagination ever busy with the old world. . . . Through all my battlings and miseries I have always lived more in the past than in the present."

To all this there is only one answer. Nobody
but himself hindered Gissing from being a scholar,
from dwelling within the walls of a college, from
amassing knowledge and living in the past. At
school and at Owen's College he showed great
promise, he won prizes and scholarships, anything
was in his grasp; he threw all away, and never
ceased to lament.

His best book I have left to the last—*By the Ionian
Sea*, which he calls " Notes of a ramble in Southern
Italy." I have read this solemn, sad and wistful
chant again and again, never tiring, and I have
lately re-read it in the delicate edition published by
Mr. Mosher of Maine. In a Foreword Mr. Mosher
says—

" It has long been in my heart to bring out *By
the Ionian Sea* in the series including *Earthwork
Out of Tuscany*, *Studies in the Renaissance*, and
Roses of Pæstum ; for I do not know of four other
volumes that could be read compelling our attention
by such associated loveliness of subject and of
style."

By the Ionian Sea is a book to read and linger over,
chapter by chapter from Paola to Reggio, and there,
on the last page is his valediction—unhappy, happy
George Gissing.

" Alone and quiet, I heard the washing of the
waves; I saw the evening fall on cloud-wreathed
Etna, the twinkling lights come forth upon Scylla
and Charybdis ; and, as I looked my last toward the
Ionian Sea, I wished it were mine to wander endlessly amid the silence of the ancient world, to-day
and all its sounds forgotten."

I see him a grave, remote, supple, inward-peering figure, as in William Rothenstein's drawing, wandering for ever through silent, classical, dateless landscapes—lakes, hills, and broken temples—such as Emil Ménard has painted.

XXIII. JOEL CHANDLER HARRIS

WE were driving across Hyde Park on the wide, twisty, leafy road that runs from Kensington to Bayswater. As we left the bridge that crosses the Serpentine and approached the Magazine, I saw in a hollow to the right, which is a kind of natural amphitheatre, a vast concourse of people—probably 5000. They were standing and reclining in a circle : all were looking down upon a stage ; but the boards were of green grass, and the stage seats were logs of wood, as in the Forest of Arden, and the dressing-rooms were tents ; and there was an orchestra playing a merry, lilting air (women performers) and a chorus, half a hundred I should think, clad in the kind of woodland raiment that Robin Hood and his Merry Men wore ; and all this within sight of Westminster Towers, and close to the motor buses and cabs that rush along Kensington Road.

"A Pastoral Play in Hyde Park," said Belinda. "England is moving with the times."

I did not answer her immediately because I had caught sight on the green stage, surrounded by ancient oaks, of two or three queer figures, neither men nor animals, yet looking something like men, and something like animals. I am, as you know, rather quick, and the advantage of Belinda as a companion is that I can say anything to her, so I remarked, with a laugh, " Looks to me like old Brer Fox and Brer Rabbit." " Don't be silly," said Belinda, " and do tell the man to hurry. It's twenty-five minutes to eight, and dinner is at half-past seven. You are incorrigible."

I made no reply because I had been ready in excellent time—I always am—but as being late for dinner is a tragedy, I said no more about Brer Fox and Brer Rabbit—forgot all about them, and regretted that I had made such a silly remark, for what connection can there be between Brer Rabbit and Brer Fox, and Hyde Park at the height of the London season ?

The odd thing is that I was right, beautifully, candidly, and consequentially right as Henry James might say. For the next morning the principal newspapers had long and charming accounts of the performance headed " *Brer Rabbit* in Hyde Park : Brer Rabbit and Mr. Fox, New Setting for an Old Story," and one of the reports ran, " The most beautifully appointed theatre in England was thrown open yesterday afternoon and evening, and the play was *Brer Rabbit.* What more fitting stage could be found for it ? Joel Chandler Harris was a genius in his way."

What memories have I of him ? Of himself—nothing : of his books—much. That is as it should be. And yet " Uncle Remus " has been for years so companionable and delightful a person that I seem to know him better than many people whom I meet constantly. *Uncle Remus : His Songs and His Sayings* (1880), *Nights with Uncle Remus* (1883), *Uncle*

Remus and His Friends (1897), *Told by Uncle Remus* (1906). I know that Uncle Remus was invented by Joel Chandler Harris, but one always thinks of them as one and the same person. Why not ?

" ' Didn't the Fox never catch the Rabbit, Uncle Remus ? ' asked the little boy.

" ' He come mighty nigh it, honey, sho's you bawn—Brer Fox did. One day atter Brer Rabbit fool 'im wid dat calamus root, Brer Fox went ter wuk en got 'im some tar, en mix it wid some turpentine, en fix up a contrapshun what he call a Tar-Baby. . . .'

" ' It's a mighty purty tale ' (Cinderella, which the little boy had told him), said Uncle Remus. ' It's so purty dat you dunner whedder ter b'lieve it er not. Yit I speck it's so, keze one time in forty lev'm hundred matters will turn out right een' upperds.' "

Uncle Remus and his talking animals have passed into the language. They are the parents of numerous books in this kind and I do not suppose that anyone, not even Kipling, has worked this genre better than Joel Chandler Harris. How much is his own invention, and how much he gleaned and adapted from the old Negro folk-lore is one of those questions that can never be adequately answered. He has been called " The Æsop of Georgia," and Brer Rabbit is a household word throughout the English-speaking world. I remember a violent discussion between two Dons as to whether it was Tar-Baby or Brer Fox who lay low and said nuthin'. They should have been better informed. Every

child knows that. " Tar-Baby ain't sayin' nuthin',
en Brer Fox, he lay low. . . . Brer Rabbit keep
on axin' 'im, en de Tar-Baby she keep on sayin'
nuthin'. . . ." And I remember a noble lord, in
a political speech, adapting the brier-patch story to
some burning question of the day. " Den Brer
Rabbit talk mighty 'umble. ' I don't keer wat
you do wid me, Brer Fox,' sezee, ' so you don't
fling me in dat brier-patch. . . .' " Then the
climax. " ' Bred en bawn in a brier-patch, Brer
Fox, bred en bawn in a brier-patch ! ' en wid
dat he skip out des ez lively ez a cricket in de
embers."

Joel Chandler Harris (1848–1908) lived most of
his life at Atlanta, Georgia. Apart from his books
his journalistic career seems to have been spent on
the *Atlanta Constitution*, of which he rose to be
editor. His recreations are recorded thus : " Thinking of things and tending his roses. Lived in the
suburb, where he had a comfortable home built to a
veranda, on a five-acre lot full of birds, flowers,
children and collards." A jolly, understanding,
sympathetic man !

I learnt, with joy, that " Brer Rabbit and Mr.
Fox," a Musical Frolic by Mabel Dearmer, with
music by Martin Shaw, was to be repeated on the
following Saturday, and that these Hyde Park enter-
tainments, " Plays for the People," are planned and
carried out by a society called the " League of Arts,"
which has, wonderful to relate, obtained permission
from His Majesty's Office of Works to perform open-
air plays and operas in the natural amphitheatre by
the Serpentine.

Would you like to see a list of the characters?
To many in England and America they will recall
happy memories.

Brer Bear	Mr. Kildee
Brer Fox	Miss Meadows
Brer Rabbit	Miss Motts
Brer Tarrypin	Miss Lucy
Brer Bullfrog	Miss Tilda
Miss Goose	Miss Nancy
King Deer	Sindy Ann
King Deer's Daughter	Rab
Mr. Man	Tobe
Miss Janey	Molly Cotton Tail

The scene is—A Woodland Glade.   For two hours
we were with Uncle Remus of Atlanta, Georgia—
he who lived in a five-acre lot full of birds, flowers,
children and collards—on, on to the end of the
frolic, with Brer Rabbit saying (see the Book of
Words), " No, no, ladies, Brer Rabbit's nobody—de
littlest of all de animals—dis (pointing to Uncle
Remus) am de author of de play."

Then a little wind rose in the trees, and the still,
clear July night began to settle down upon London.
But I did not hear the hoot of the motors, did not
see the policeman on point duty rigidly holding back
the crowd, for I was seeing a sleepy little boy sitting
with Uncle Remus in a veranda in Georgia, and the
little boy is saying—

" The Bear didn't catch the Rabbit, then? "

And Uncle Remus answers—

" Jump up fum dar, honey. I ain't got no

time fer ter be settin' yer proppin' yo' eyeleds open."

From Georgia to London! From London to Georgia! In an intonation, in the twinkling of an eye, imagination leaps the miles.

XXIV. W. H. HUDSON

SOME years ago on a walk through Kent, I called upon a critic-naturalist who had built himself a back-to-the-land house in the least spoiled and most inaccessible spot of southern England. We were standing at the edge of his rough but reasoned garden, which rambles off into a wood, and I was talking of Tennyson's knowledge of nature, and slowly becoming aware that my Thoreau-like friend was not listening to me. He said, "Oh," and "Indeed," and "Surely"; but his attention was with his eyes, which were fixed on a tall, sturdy, free-moving figure, meandering around a pond, visible through the wood. Sometimes this lonely individual would stoop and gaze intently into the still water, pick something out and examine it; then he would rise from his haunches and resume his slow, peering ramble around the insignificant pond.

I passed from Tennyson to make a remark or two about the latest volume in the Pseudonym Library, but my friend still continued to give me but half his attention. At last I said petulantly—even philosophers are petulant sometimes—"What's the matter? Why does your mind wander? What are you looking at?"

Still with his eyes on the pond he answered, "That's W. H. Hudson. He's studying newts.

Hudson is a great man." Then he looked a little
pathetically at me, and his look seemed to say,
" You're a little man. That is why I am giving my
attention to Hudson."

Would you believe it, that rural episode set me
slightly against Hudson. I was young. My friend
the critic-naturalist was one of a coterie who, as the
years passed, adopted the rôle of a W. H. Hudson
admiration society. For a decade and more he had
been neglected by the general public, and this little
coterie, which plumed itself upon being wiser and
more perceptive than the general, talked up and
wrote up Hudson, and hailed him as a Great Man
until I became as tired of hearing him called Great,
as the Athenians were of hearing Aristides called
Just. I feel this way about Joseph Conrad, whom
it is now the fashion to extol extremely. Of course
I should like such a thing to happen to myself; but
I, like most readers, prefer to form my own judg-
ments about authors.

I do not blame Hudson for the worship of his
admirers. He is the most modest and retiring of
men. You rarely meet him at functions; he prefers nature to man, and he had such a long period of
neglect that a little overpraise will not hurt him.
But has he been overpraised? That question has
been troubling me during the past week, which I
have spent reconsidering Hudson.

I have only seen him twice—at the newt pond,
and in 1907 when he was writing *The Land's End :
a Naturalist's Impressions in West Cornwall.* We
met under curious conditions on the bleak hills
above Zennor, near the Land's End, and I eyed him

with interest, because I was also writing a book on
Cornwall. As I am neither a hawk, nor a newt, nor
an armadillo he did not pay any attention to me.
We passed each other gruffly, he studying—gulls and
robins, I—stone circles and cromlechs. When his
book appeared the last paragraph made me rather
angry. He seems to resent the acquisition of the
Rokeby " Venus " by Velasquez for the National
Gallery, because the money, he thinks, might have
been better spent in making the Land's End a
National possession. That is like mayors in America
who resent fine buildings and the acquisition of
fine pictures, because the money could be spent on
bathing beaches and homes for the poor.

I do not think *The Land's End* one of his best
books ; but as the years passed I began to realize
that, in spite of the overpraise of his admirers,
Hudson is a beautiful and exceptional writer, with
a great power of observation, and the ability to
express himself in melodious, unaffected prose. He
seems to write with the ease of a bird singing, and
his thoughts are his own thoughts : always lonely,
yet happy. I realized that I must write about
him.

That adventure was forced on me when I read
this in *The Dial* by Ford Madox Hueffer—" We
wanted to write, I suppose, as only Mr. W. H.
Hudson writes—as simply as the grass grows." " Ho,
ho ! " I said. " Here is another admirer, a new member of the coterie. What is there about Hudson
that makes critics stand on their toes and shout ?
Shall I be doing it before I am through with
him ? "

The next thing was to read *Green Mansions*, which my bookseller told me had gone through nine printings since 1916. So I bought it. I am very human. I took it away into the country, and read it in bed in the morning, and under a tree in the afternoon.

It is introduced with a Foreword by John Galsworthy which, if I were in the habit of using slang, I should say made me "sit up." The praise of Hudson of the others is as nothing compared with that of Galsworthy. Here are a few sentences— " As a simple narrator he is well-nigh unsurpassed ; as a stylist he has few, if any, living equals. . . . Of all living authors—now that Tolstoy has gone I could least dispense with W. H. Hudson. . . . A very great writer : and—to my thinking—the most valuable our Age possesses."

I enjoyed *Green Mansions* immensely, but it would have pleased me better if it had not been in the form of fiction. I believe Hudson when he tells me his own thoughts, observations and reflections ; but he does not convince me when he uses Mr. Abel as a mouthpiece. In a word I want Hudson pure, not Hudson clothed with the stock garments of fiction.

So with *The Purple Land* and *A Crystal Age*. To me they have an air of unreality that is so perfectly absent from Hudson's personal books. Theodore Roosevelt adds himself to the list of Hudson's admirers in " An Introductory Note " to *The Purple Land*—" His writings come in that very small class of books which deserve the title of literature," and so on. And Barrie says—" It is one of the choicest things of our latter-day literature." They all love Hudson.

Roosevelt also praises " those delightful books," *Idle Days in Patagonia* and *The Naturalist in La Plata*. There I am entirely with him : such as these are the real Hudson. When I read his books about nature (he loves everything, even snakes and spiders) I feel myself being drawn into the Hudson coterie. I want to express my gratitude, and to praise him.

I go through his nature books and re-read the passages I have marked. This to children in *Hampshire Days*—" Pet nothing, persecute nothing " ; this in *Nature in Downland*—" Here, sitting on the dry grass with my face to the wind, I spent two or three hours in gazing at the thistle-down " ; this from *Adventures Among Birds*—" I could hear the wind in the bulrushes, miles on miles of dark polished stems, tufted with ruddy brown ; that low, mysterious sound is to me the most fascinating of all the many voices of the wind."

A remote, wandering man is W. H. Hudson, here to-day, gone to-morrow, off to some new adventure with nature, leaving no postal address. Little is known about the events of his life, little has he told ; but he has said that he has had no career— " just a drifting along," and this—" All the interesting part of my life ended when I ceased to be a boy, and my autobiography ends at fifteen."

That wonderful boyhood is told in *Far Away and Long Ago*, the story of his early life on the South American pampas, and his awakening to the eternal interest and endless consolation of nature. This to

L

me is his most beautiful and interesting book, this story of his wonderful boyhood.

Come to think of it, I was happy in my two encounters with this naturalist, for on each occasion I saw him absorbed in nature—peering into the pond in Kent, and gazing at the gulls over Cornwall.

XXV. A. S. M. HUTCHINSON

BY a happy chance it was Sinclair Lewis, author of *Main Street*, who introduced me to A. S. M. Hutchinson, author of *If Winter Comes*. The significance of this episode may not be apparent to Oxford Dons, or Appalachian mountaineers; but to a Bookman its remarkable significance is that one " best seller " introduced me to another " best seller."

How strange it is, and how encouraging that the two best sellers of the day should be two such fine books as *Main Street* and *If Winter Comes*, one dealing with life in an American new, small town, the other in and around an old English village. In each the characters are real and human, and each book has sold, I am told, more than a quarter of a million copies in America, with innumerable printings in England and Canada. One who knows tells me that *If Winter Comes* may reach a sale of half a million copies.

So it was interesting to see these two young authors together, and to find these " best sellers " enthusiastic about each other's work—the American tall, slim, blond, alert, with easy movements and quick eyes, noting things in a flash and directly: the Englishman slim, pale, reflective rather than alert, with the almost shy look of a man who absorbs before he expresses himself, and then obliquely rather than directly. He wears glasses.

It is the literary paragraphists of the press who foster the interest of the public in " best sellers." Items detailing the number of printings, accounts of the presses running night and day, calculations of sales at the rate of " three copies a minute," make " good copy." For everyone is interested in success. No doubt the send-off of *If Winter Comes* was helped by Sir James Barrie, who wrote to the author : " Please let a fellow-writer congratulate you very heartily on *If Winter Comes*, the best novel I had read for many a day." This frank praise from a great and kindly fellow-worker has, strange to say, crept into the advertisements.

I, in common with others, perused these paragraphs, and, like others, I began to wonder why this book should be so popular, for of a hundred novels published most fall flat, a few have a tolerable success, but here was one with a success that might almost be called unparalleled. I became curious about A. S. M. Hutchinson, and wondered if he was in *Who's Who*.

He is. He comes of good stock—military-writing stock ; his father is Lieut.-Gen. H. D. Hutchinson, a distinguished retired Anglo-Indian soldier, and author of such books as *Military Sketching Made Easy* and *The Campaign in Tirah*. The author of *If Winter Comes* was born at Gorakpur, India, in 1879. He was educated in Kent, at St. Lawrence College, Thanet ; then he studied medicine, abandoned it, and took to writing, the journalistic branch, which for beginners is the paying branch,

worked with the Pearson firm, and became editor
of the *Daily Graphic* in 1912. I wonder if he
wrote the editorials that I used to admire so much
in that bright illustrated daily.

His experiences in the Great War made him feel
that he never wanted to write again, but once a
writer always a writer. Although he may have
felt at the time that he would never write again,
the story of *If Winter Comes* buried itself in his
brain during the war days, developed itself, and
when peace came it " suddenly demanded to be
written. More. It wrote itself."

The strange and happy thing about *If Winter
Comes* is that there is no attempt in it to please,
or to write down to the public. The opening
chapter wherein the " garrulous Hapgood " is
allowed to introduce the chief character, is of a
kind, crabbed and oblique, that might baulk those
novel-readers—and they are the majority—who like
the primrose way, easy-chair method of introducing
a character. But the passionate sincerity of the
analysis gets hold of the reader, and he soon feels
an intense sympathy for Mark Sabre, the hero,
a twentieth-century example of the good man
struggling against adversity.

This man, this Mark Sabre, who has the habit
" of seeing things from about twenty points of view
instead of one," is an essential Truth-seeker who
wars not against principalities and powers, but
against convention, stupidity and selfishness in
the people of his environment. Or rather they
war against him. And they are not abstractions :
they are not stage dummies : they are very real

people, so real, so natural, the pleasant ones as well
as the unpleasant ones, that I am inclined to think
that Mr. Hutchinson's greatest gift is his power of
vivid characterization, which is, of course, the hall-
mark of all the great writers of fiction. If I were
a preacher I would be disposed to say that the fact
of half a million of people having read and liked
this book is a sure sign of the rightness of the reading
world, and a most encouraging sign of the times.
Idealism, and the scent, unerring when it is really
there, for righteousness is stronger to-day than
ever.

I must copy a passage from *If Winter Comes*.
It shows the author's quick style, the flashlight of
his revelation of character, and his tuition.

" One evening he asked her a most extraordinary
question, shot out of him without intending it,
discharged out of his questing thoughts as by a
hidden spring suddenly touched by groping fingers.

" ' Effie, do you love God ? '

" Her surprise seemed to him to be more at the
thing he had asked than at its amazing unexpected-
ness and amazing irrelevancy. ' Why, of course I
do, Mr. Sabre.'

" ' Why do you ? '

" She was utterly at a loss. ' Well, of course
I do.'

" He said rather sharply, ' Yes, but *why* ? Have
you ever asked yourself why ? Respecting, fearing,
trusting, that's understandable. But love, *love ;*
you know what love is, don't you ? What's love
got to do with God ? '

" She said in simple wonderment, as one asked

what had the sun to do with light, or whether water was wet, ' Why, God *is* love.'

" He stared at her."

And we are told that " nothing of that wanting-something look " was ever to be seen in Effie's shining eyes. She had the secret of life.

The title-page of *If Winter Comes* describes A. S. M. Hutchinson as also the author of *The Happy Warrior, Once Aboard the Lugger,* and *The Clean Heart.* I have read *The Happy Warrior.* It is a fine book, with characters in it that are Dickensian in their ready humour and lusty characterization; but it has not the maturity or reasoned development of *If Winter Comes.*

The Bookman magazine designed an original competition. It offered prizes for the best answers to two questions suggested by *If Winter Comes.* Mr. Hutchinson read and judged the answers. Has this ever happened before ?

Publishers are naturally interested in the success of *If Winter Comes.* One of them said to me, " My dear sir, it means a small fortune for the author, and—ahem—for the publisher, and a straight run into success for Hutchinson's next books, and certainly for *This Freedom.*"

" Would you have prophesied the success of *If Winter Comes* ? " I asked.

He shook his head. " No one can forecast what the reception of a novel or a play will be ? With Essays it is easy."

" Yes," I said, " with Essays it is easy."

XXVI. FORD MADOX HUEFFER

I HAVE not seen Ford Madox Hueffer since the second year of the war, when I met him, one Sunday afternoon, walking in Hyde Park with Wyndham Lewis. He told me that he had "joined up." As his volume of poems called *On Heaven, and Poems written on Active Service* is dedicated to the commander of the Welch Regiment, I presume it was the Welch Regiment that he joined. Without doubt he was a good soldier. He wrote a clever novel called *The Good Soldier*, which many people bought thinking it was the kind of book that Donald Hankey writes. They are very different.

Ford Madox Hueffer is always having little, round-the-corner successes. *On Heaven* appeared in *Poetry* of Chicago, and *Antwerp* was first published by the "Poetry Bookshop." The book contains one of those "provocative prefaces" which Mr. Hueffer likes writing. He announces that *vers libre* is the only medium in which he can convey his intimate moods, and adds : "*Vers libre* is a very jolly medium in which to write and to read, if it be read conversationally and quietly." I thinks he makes verse and writes prose rather easily. He turns without effort from *When Blood is Their Argument : An Analysis of Prussian Culture* to *Zeppelin Nights*, a series of short stories set in

every period of English history.   And I have heard
a whisper that Daniel Chaucer, author of *The Simple
Life Limited* and *The New Humpty Dumpty*, is Ford
Madox Hueffer.   A versatile man !

He loves to expound the art of writing and the
art of great writers, such as Henry James, whom he
admires immensely;   so when he takes pen in hand
he is ready for the tripping, reasoned words.   Yes,
he likes *vers libre :* it enables him to make definite
statements like this—

> " About the middle of my first Last Leave,
>   I stood on the curb in the pitch of the night
>   Waiting for the buses that didn't come
>   To take me home.
>   That was in Paddington.
>   The soot-black night was over one like velvet,
>   And one was very alone—so very alone
>   In the velvet cloak of the night."

He published his *Collected Poems* in 1914, and
if ever he issues a uniform edition of his prose works
it will need a long, long shelf to hold them, for he
has written many books on many subjects : he has
written on art, criticism, topography, history, with
gay excursions into fiction.   He has also written
Memories.

To me his Memories are his most interesting
books;   and if he seems a little weary of the whole
business, a little querulous, and disposed to think
writing, like everything else, somewhat of a bore,
we must not mind.   It is only his way.   He is
somewhat tired of greatness and great men.   He
was nourished on them.   It was not his fault.

He is a grandson of Ford Madox Brown.   The

great men who congregated around that great man, at the great, gaunt house (pleasant enough in the studio) in Fitzroy Square, encircled him from babyhood. Is that an advantage, or a disadvantage? I know not; but it certainly has had a marked effect on the life of Ford Madox Hueffer. Oh, and his father was Dr. Francis Hueffer, the celebrated musical critic of *The Times*.

In the dedication to "My Dear Kids," his daughters Christine and Katherine, that prefaces his volume of *Memories* of the Pre-Raphaelite and Æsthetic Movements, he plays amusingly, but not without hints of self-pity, on the drawback of being brought up among great men. He tells of the Eminent Ones who came to his grandfather's house and how these "Victorian great figures" always seemed to be twenty-five feet high, and himself, as his father once called him, "the patient but extremely stupid donkey." In this environment he learnt to regard himself as the most obscure of obscure persons. "To me life was simply not worth living because of the existence of Carlyle, of Mr. Ruskin, of Mr. Holman Hunt, of Mr. Browning, or of the gentlemen who built the Crystal Palace. These people were perpetually held up to me as standing upon unattainable heights, and at the same time I was perpetually being told that if I could not attain these heights I might just as well not cumber the earth. What, then, was left for me? Nothing. Simply nothing."

The world went quietly on, and as he grew up he discovered that it is by no means populated with great Victorians, that all people are not Rossettis

and Ruskins, and that all grandfathers are not Ford
Madox Browns. But he has never quite overcome
his veneration for the Eminent, and when I first
knew him many years ago he chided me one day for
saying something human about Henry James and
Swinburne. " You mustn't talk about Great Men in
that intimate way," he said, with the tired smile, half
amusement, half petulance, that he usually employs.

His manner is never corybantic, and when he
told me that afternoon in Hyde Park that he had
" joined up," he did so with the air of saying that
he had changed houses. I have seen nothing of
him since that day, but he came vividly before me
when I opened *The Dial* and found that he had been
invited by the editor to write his reminiscences.
The editor asked him formally to treat seventeen
British contemporaries, and added, as an after-
thought—" also Rudyard Kipling and any of *les
jeunes* that you like."

That gave Fordie (thus his grandfather called
him, and I maintain that he has not yet quite grown
up) his chance. He begins his reminiscences thus—
" It is twenty-two years and six months since, at
Michaelmas, 1897, I received a letter from Mr.
Conrad, asking me to collaborate with him." Mr.
Conrad has yet to explain why he chose Mr. Hueffer.
Henley may have had something to do with it.

Conrad was not then a great man, but he was
shaping for one, so you see how the society of the
Great pursues the grandson of Ford Madox Brown.
That afternoon when I met him in Hyde Park he
was walking with Wyndham Lewis.

The collaboration resulted, as everyone knows,

in *Romance* and *The Inheritors*, not outstanding books ; indeed Mr. Hueffer says frankly—" I fancy that neither book has any artistic value at all." What then was the purpose of the collaboration ? I suppose to teach Conrad English, for at that time, on his own confession, he thought in Polish, expressed himself in French, and only with difficulty " rendered his thus-worded French thoughts and images in English." Mr. Hueffer was sure that he understood the art of expression in words. Has he not said—" I am alone among English-born writers to bother my head primarily about the ' how ' of writing " ? You perceive that Mr. Hueffer has quite overcome his Fitzroy Square timidity and self-depression. You must read this first chapter of his Memoirs ; how he and Conrad studied Flaubert, Flaubert, Flaubert and, buried " in rural greennesses," had endless discussions on how to write. " I think that I was most preoccupied with the expression of fine shades ; Conrad's unceasing search in those days was for a new form of novel. But I do not believe that there were in the England of those days any two other people whose whole minds and whose unceasing endeavours were so absolutely given to that one problem of expression between man and man which is the end of all conscious literary art."

Of the many books that Ford Madox Hueffer has written I like best, after his *Memories*, the volumes on art, and on places, such as *The Soul of London* and *England and the English*. That romantic novel, *The Half Moon*, which begins at Rye, in Sussex, and ends with Henry Hudson sailing up to Albany, might have been a great romance. Does it fail because the author is convinced that the manner of literature is so much more important than the matter?

He is a curious mixture of modesty and effrontery. In conversation he is modest; with a pen in his hand he sometimes writes in a way that goads the average man to exasperation. The article in *The Dial* is a case in point. Some find it interesting and amusing; others, when half-way through, fling the magazine across the room.

Obviously a man of talent and learning, some of his friends sometimes try to check his ambient air of knowing everything. Years ago when I was staying at Winchelsea I told a lady that I was about to spend the evening at the Hueffers'. "Don't praise Fordie to his face," she said. "It's not good for him." In the course of the evening someone sang what I thought was an Elizabethan song very beautifully. The strong and lyrical simplicity of the words were wedded to an air that suited them exactly. I was so charmed with the performance that I begged for a repetition. This was done, and I said, with some emotion, and not without pride in my perspicacity : "What a combination—Shakespeare and Purcell. We can do nothing like that nowadays."

Fordie, who had been reclining on a couch, suppressed a yawn and said, " I wrote the words and the music."

.   .   .   .   .

I read the above article to a friend of Fordie's. When it was finished I said : " Do you think he will be pleased with it ? "

" Not terribly," she answered.

" Anyhow, he gets a whole article about himself,"
I replied.

. . . . .

He has now, I believe, retired into the country,
and he has told his friends that he is through with
literature and finds consolation in Adam's profession.
That, I fancy, is only a mood. Once a writer,
always a writer.

XXVII. JAMES GIBBONS HUNEKER

SOME years ago, a Baltimore friend sent me to London a copy of *Promenades of an Impressionist*, by James Gibbons Huneker. I read it with amazement. " Do all up-to-date Americans write like this ? " I asked myself.

Such a dazzle of a style ; such a pepper of names ; such a hulloa-old-chap familiarity with Eminent Hands in the Seven Arts, mostly foreign ; such staccato sentences, such high spirits, such a gusto for life. It was unlike any other book I had ever read, and although I should not like all literature to be written in the Huneker manner, I was delighted to make acquaintance with *Promenades of an Impressionist*. It braced me, made me hustle, and I wondered what Dr. Johnson would have thought of Huneker's American style.

" No," said a compatriot of Huneker's, " all Americans do not write like Jim. He's just Jim Huneker, who collects artistic reputations, pins them down like so many butterflies, and he's so enthusiastic about everything that the pins don't seem to hurt. He's antibunk, is Jim."

Pursuing my investigations into the Huneker concatenations I found the following in *The Athenæum* apropos *New Cosmopolis :* " Given a different environment, another training, Mr. Huneker might have emerged as an American Walter Pater."

Has a great journal ever said anything so silly? James Huneker could never have been anything but James Huneker: as for training, he trained himself, just in the way he wanted to be trained; as for environment, he made himself a citizen of the world. This "gourmet of belles-lettres," as a French critic called him, dedicated to a "half-mad worship of the Seven Arts," was as unlike Pater as Henry James was dissimilar to O. Henry. Walter Pater may be likened to a gentleman-farmer, quiet and thoughtful, brooding on his fields, watching his crops, sensitive to their nourishment and growth, with occasional reflective glances at sky and birds. Huneker is a keen-eyed traveller flashing past on a motor bicycle, waving a greeting to the reflective husbandman as he whizzes toward the next town.

The capitals of the world were Huneker's real homes—the Opera House, the Concert Rooms, the Theatres, Studios and Salons.

Pater is—repose. Huneker is—rush. He was a true American. His curiosity was insatiable. From Walt Whitman to Mary Garden, what an array of distinguished people he knew, remembered and wrote about. His style glitters, jumps, turns back, doubles in its tracks. He likes the short sentence. Thus—

"We must believe in the reality of our Unicorn. He is Pan. He is Puck. He is Shelley. He is Ariel. He is Whim. He is Irony."

James Gibbons Huneker was a protagonist of the Seven Arts: Music, Literature, Painting, Sculpture, Architecture, Acting, Dancing, but his first love and his last was Music. In *Unicorns* he

writes, " Music-mad, I arrived in Paris during the
last weeks of the World's Fair of 1878, impelled
there by a parching desire to see Franz Liszt, if not
to hear him." Note the use of the word " parching."
That was Huneker. He would always rather be
shrill than whisper. Imagine a shrill Walter Pater !

He was an inspired journalist, a literary journalist
who, like many other brilliant writers, Chesterton
for example, do their best work against time, when
forced to concentrate by the approach of the publication hour. His *Life of Chopin*, probably his
best performance, and already a classic, was produced
at leisure, as Pater composed. Huneker was bound
to write a fine book on Chopin. He adored him,
played him, understood him. In *The Pathos of
Distance*, which contains a chapter on his first visit
to Paris in the seventies, he writes—

" I had mastered a page of Chopin ; I was happy ;
I was in Paris ; I was young. And being of a practical temperament, I read Browning every morning
to prepare myself for the struggle with the world."

There speaks the young American—of a past
decade. Other times, other ways.

Never have I been able to recapture the enthusiasm
with which I read *Promenades of an Impressionist*.
The Huneker method becomes a little tiring. His
attack is always frontal, never round through the
sympathies. The way to read him is the way of
reading " O. Henry," in single instalments of a
column or so in a daily newspaper. Once, in an
article by Huneker I counted nineteen names,
all of exclusive men, working in the Seven Arts.
One had to read him carefully.

M

Such articles were too good to be lost. Hence the procession of Huneker books, consisting of short essays on Men, Women, Cities, Ideas and Fancies linked under fanciful titles. In his titles, as in his style, he never rests. Here are a few of them—

Overtures—A Book of Temperaments, essays mainly on music, with this quotation from Whitman on the title-page : " Do I contradict myself ? Very well, then, I contradict myself " ; *Mezzotints*, more about music with a long essay on " The Music of the Future " ; *Unicorns*, with essays on Cézanne, James Joyce, Creative Involution and Re-reading Mallock ; *Egoists, a Book of Supermen*, with a quotation from Goethe on the title-page ; *Iconoclasts, a Book of Dramatists* from Ibsen to Shaw, with the motto " My truth is the truth " ; *Ivory, Apes, and Peacocks*, the title from 2 Chronicles ix. 21, all about authors and painters ; *New Cosmopolis, a Book of Images*, interpreting cities, with an Italian quotation on the title-page ; *Bedouins*, mainly about Mary Garden, but also about George Luks, and Calico Cats, and Caruso on Wheels ; and with a section called " Idols and Ambergris " ; and so on. There was no end to Huneker's fecundity and faithfulness to æsthetic excitement.

Of all his books I prefer the volume of short stories called *Visionaries*. He had no skill in characterization, but he had ideas, quick, odd and fourth dimensional. Sometimes this player with words descends to a quiet passage : it is very welcome. Pater might almost have written the following. It occurs in the essay on " The Artist and His Wife."

"The true artist temperament, in reality, is the perception and appreciation of beauty whether in pigment, form, tone, words, or in nature. It may exist coevally with a strong religious sense."

Huneker published his autobiography in two volumes. Characteristically he called it *Steeplejack* with this explanation : " I, who write these words, am no poet, but I have been a steeplejack. I have climbed to the very top of many steeples the world over, and dreamed like the rest of my fellow-beings the dreams that . . ."

It is a jolly book, ill-shaped, but lively and curiously confidential. It should have been longer, or it should have been shorter, which you will. In it I find hints that, like other literary men who have lived by journalism, he had, now and then, a passing regret that he did not devote himself entirely to creative work, to writing grave things, like Pater, in the leisure of ample mornings. Who knows ? Probably we all do what we were meant to do, and what we can best do. But—(this from *Steeplejack*)—

" I love painting and sculpture. I may only look, but never own either pictures or marbles. I would fain be a pianist, a composer of music. I am neither. Nor a poet. Nor a novelist, actor, playwright. I have written of many things, from architecture to zoology, without grasping their inner substance. I am Jack of the Seven Arts, master of none. A steeplejack of the arts."

James Gibbons Huneker ran true to form. Music was his first love and his last, and his idol from first to last was Chopin ; perhaps he never expressed

himself so completely as in the concluding lines of
Steeplejack.

"What shall I do? Music, always music. There
are certain compositions by my beloved Chopin to
master which eternity itself would not be too long.
. . . Courage! Time is fugacious. How many
years have I not played that magic music? Music
the flying vision . . . music that merges with the
tender air . . . its image melts on shy, misty
shadows . . . the cloud, the cloud, the singing,
shining cloud . . . over the skies and far away . . .
the beckoning clouds. . . ."

There Huneker speaks, he himself.

XXVIII. VICENTE BLASCO IBÁÑEZ

WHEN I was in New York the papers announced in bold type that Vicente Blasco Ibáñez was "preparing to write a novel about America." This ardent Spanish writer and publicist does not know English, but " the greatest of living novelists " (*vide* the advertisements of his clever publishers) rises above such a slight limitation. A few months of rapid observation and travel, a few months of rushing writing, and the book will be done. We shall all be reading it. His publishers will see to that. They have exploited Ibáñez magnificently. By the cleverest advertising campaign that has come under my notice, outspoken and intelligent as well as clever, they forced America to take Ibáñez to its fireside. For weeks I resisted the blandishments of their advertisements, as I resisted the advertisements of a suit of B. V. D. underwear and an electric toaster; but in the end I was conquered. Advertisement always conquers, provided that the article advertised is worthy. Meekly I bought *The Four Horsemen of the Apocalypse* and read it : meekly I bought *The Shadow of the Cathedral* and read it, and it only needed a few more thousand dollars of expert advertising to make me buy *Mare Nostrum, Blood and Sand*, and *La Bodega*.

Do I think Ibáñez the greatest of living novelists ? Well, no ! There is a shy, sad man living in Dorset-

shire, England, called Thomas Hardy; there are
others, a dozen and more : there is the author of
Kim, and *Captains Courageous;* there is Conrad.
A man does not become a tremendous novelist
because he handles tremendous themes. The soul,
as Maeterlinck observes, does not always flower on
nights of storm.

Does Ibáñez (see advertisements) " scatter the
riches of his imagination with a prodigality like
that of Balzac or Dumas " ? Does he " paint great
subjects on big canvases, with the sweep of a master " ?
I will disregard Balzac and Dumas. Ibáñez certainly paints great subjects on big canvases. But
has he the " sweep of a master " ? Well, no.

In my opinion *The Shadow of the Cathedral* is a
much finer book than *The Four Horsemen.* It
shapes better, and the theme, a devastating indict-
ment, is logically and comprehensively worked out.
But *The Shadow of the Cathedral* would never have
had its present success had it not been for the " big
boom " (do you remember Stephen Leacock's
delightful irony about the word " big " in criticism ?)
in *The Four Horsemen.* Why was that work so
successful ? Fifty per cent. of its success, perhaps
more, was due to clever advertising; but *The Four
Horsemen* also galloped up Fifth Avenue at the
psychological moment. The war was at its height,
the newspapers were crowded with bewildering
details, the tongues of gossips ran ceaselessly, everybody was feverish for news, many little, jumpy
men wrote long, jumpy articles, and into this
hubbub of sketches rolled the big (I must use the
word) crude canvas of *The Four Horsemen of the*

Apocalypse. Obviously the author is a vital man, a man of parts and energy, who had seen the war, who had felt its horror and sorrow, who has a big (forgive me) surging imagination, so riotous that while he is composing he is quite unable to pause anywhere for art's sake. " I write explosively," says Ibáñez. " I am sometimes hardly aware what I am doing. The germ of an idea comes to me ; it grows and grows until there is a sort of spontaneous combustion." Just so. That is the reason why I prefer Mrs. Burnett or Edith Wharton, Barrie or Leonard Merrick.

Ibáñez begins a novel slowly, he climbs laboriously, he reaches the crest, then " once on the other side I cannot stop myself—I rush headlong, whirling, plunging, working endlessly until I reach the finale." He wrote *The Four Horsemen* in four months in Paris, in 1916. Toward the end " I worked thirty hours at a stretch." This is magnificent, but it is not art. Of course I am well aware that the readers who make up the 100,000 circulation groups do not want art : they want a story. But we must keep the flag of art flying. Perhaps I should not have penned this gentle protest had not his publishers called him " the greatest of living novelists," and had they not announced in big (ah, again) type that he is " the dominant figure in the world of modern fiction."

But I do not want to belittle Ibáñez. He is a force ; he has gusto and vitality, and he is fiercely interested in many things besides the writing of fiction—politics, history, sociology. His tirade on Ponce de Léon was fine, his defence of Spain was

passionately eloquent. He is quick. When a
heckler asked him, " Why did Spain come to Mexico
to disturb the Indians ? " he answered, " Why were
the Indians of Manhattan disturbed ? " He can
make a gesture, too, as when he led the subscriptions
for a memorial in the Bronx to Edgar Allan Poe.

As Vicente Blasco Ibáñez signed a $30,000 lecture
contract in America a great many people had an
opportunity of hearing him. I had that pleasure.
The proceedings were divided into two parts.
First, a gentleman who knows both Spanish and
English read a translation of what Señor Ibáñez
was about to say. That was not very exciting,
and when the folk in the gallery shouted to him
to speak up, he was apparently unable to oblige.
Having repeated their cries of " Louder," and
" Speak up," with no effect, they stampeded down
to the balcony. That was exciting. There were
vacant chairs in the box which I occupied. Upon
them I had deposited my hat, cane, coat and a
Spanish-English dictionary. Suddenly the box was
invaded by a bevy of high-school girls from the
upper regions. They were about to take a real
Spanish lesson. From them I learnt more than
from the dictionary. Indeed, the entire audience
was very interesting. Latins permit themselves
to betray emotion, and it was a pleasure to watch
their expressive faces as Ibáñez declaimed, protested,
cajoled, persuaded and suggested.

He is an orator, a natural orator, I should say.
His gestures seem impulsive, they follow his thought,
the whole man moves as he talks, and at the right
moment he glides from one side of the reading desk

to the other. There is a manuscript on the desk;
he never refers to it; but the desk is useful to tap
upon with his long fingers when he wishes to
emphasize points. Frequent applause follows his
periods, which he utilizes to pat his brow with a
beautiful white handkerchief. When the applause
was loudest the bevy of girls informed me he had
been saying that the only thing that can drive away
Social Unrest, the " Fifth Horseman of the Apocalypse," is Social Justice. " Why cannot we unite
on justice ? " he cried. " How strange it is that
human beings who can stand shoulder to shoulder
in war should drift apart when the imminent menace
is conquered, and by their differences invite
catastrophe."

A vital, vigorous, fearless man. A sturdy man
with a bull-like head; an " agin the Government "
man : in 1885 he was imprisoned for six months
for writing a sonnet against the Spanish Government ;
a man of imagination and dynamic driving power.
My only objection to him is that he allows himself
to be called " the greatest of living novelists." But
perhaps, as he doesn't read English, he is not aware
that this has been said about him. So here's to you,
Vicente Blasco Ibáñez.

XXIX. W. W. JACOBS

IN the late nineties sometimes I met at literary
gatherings, which usually took the form of
crowded " At Homes " and dinners, a slight,
slim, unobtrusive young man, fair and clean-shaven,
with observant eyes, whose way it was to hover
shyly on the outskirts of the crowd. He did not
make much impression upon me : he never said
anything particularly witty or tender : we just
nodded, but I always seemed to know that this
hovering, unobtrusive man was present. He wrote,
I was told, funny little stories about sailormen ; but
in those days I was not interested in funny little
stories about sailormen.

I met him also at the houses of H. G. Wells and
other friends, and in the company of fellow-humorists
(those were the days of the New Humour) such as
Jerome K. Jerome, Barry Pain and W. Pett Ridge.
He never had much to say, but one was always
glad to see him. There was a companionable air
about his unchanging habit of observation, and his
silent and rather ironical attitude, which suggested
that he paid visits, and attended social gatherings
as a way of filling time, rather than as an opportunity
for studying character.

Obviously the men and women that he met on
these occasions were of little use to him in his stories.
Not one of us understood the difference between

a barque and a schooner : we knew something about
Guy de Maupassant and Flaubert, but nothing
about marline-spikes or capstans. Where W. W.
Jacobs got his intricate nautical knowledge from I
know not. He never paraded it : he never said
" Avast there " or " Shiver my timbers," and he
never, in my hearing, made any reference to that
exhaustless and amusing person—the Night Watchman—who figures in so many of his stories. He was
merely W. W. Jacobs, a silent little man with the
humorist's tell-tale mouth, who had a snug berth
as clerk in the Savings Bank Department of the
Civil Service, and who added to his income by writing
stories in the evenings.

Gradually it became borne in upon me that his
stories were important. People talked about them,
never critically, never with any idea of " placing "
him, never comparing this short story writer with
the writers of other short stories. Everybody's
attitude to a tale by W. W. Jacobs was just enjoyment. He brightened an hour : he made the
laughter ripple, and he pleased everybody. He
captured the Great Public which merely wants
to be amused, and interested the Little Public of
critics and faddists who dread being amused lest
their judgment of the correct canons of literary
art should be over-ridden by mere delight in a human
nature humorous story. Few books are welcomed
with such gusts of praise as *Many Cargoes*, his first
volume, which was issued in 1896. Who could
resist a story beginning—

" A small but strong lamp was burning in the
fo'c'sle of the schooner ' Greyhound,' by the light of

which a middle-aged seaman of sedate appearance
sat crocheting an antimacassar." There are twenty-
one stories in *Many Cargoes,* all variations on one
string, each neat, direct, humorous; and one is as
good as another.

Many people were familiar with these stories,
for many of them had appeared in *To-day* and
The Idler under Jerome K. Jerome's editorship;
and later the word went round that the astute
George Newnes was paying W. W. Jacobs enormous
sums for the stories he wrote each month for *The
Strand Magazine.* A good Jacobs sailorman story
always was, and I suppose still is, a draw. Everyone
likes to laugh, and it is impossible not to laugh when
Jacobs means us to laugh. He never bores the reader.
He makes pictures but he ignores scenery. I do
not say that all sailormen talk as amusingly in life
as the Jacobs sailormen of fiction; but the reader
feels that it is all quite natural and inevitable.
Every page has its laugh or its smile. His sentiment
is austere, and he has no sense of tears.

The Jacobs recipe is simple. First there is
characterization, whether it be a seaman, a seaman's
wife, or a pretty girl whose destiny it is to become
a seaman's wife. The dialogue is the essence of
his stories, and he never goes wrong with it. He
embroils these characters in complications; he
sets them at cross purposes, and all comes happily
right, or humorously wrong, in the end. The setting
of these tales is familiarly unfamiliar even to Londoners—the sea hamlets that spout out along the
mouth of the Thames, the inland waterways fed
by barges, and the southern and eastern coast towns,

visited by hardy sailing vessels. Sometimes his
sailormen set forth on long voyages; but our
author rarely follows them. The captains and mates
disappear, and their lives are not resumed until
they return to Fairhaven, or Wapping Old Stairs,
or Salthaven, or Limehouse or Dialstone Lane.

All this would be as nothing were it not for one
thing—the Jacobs humour. That is the cement
that unites him to all sorts and conditions of people.
It never fails him: it is as bubbling in his long
stories as in his short ones, and the only reason that
I prefer the short stories to the long ones, is that in
the short stories the humour is directer and quicker.
But even in the long stories there is no padding.
No author ever did without padding so neatly.

One complaint only I have against him. Sometimes when I have settled myself to enjoy a Jacobs
story, I find that I have slipped into reading one of
his gruesome tales such as " The Monkey's Paw "
or " The Well." They are excellently done because
he is a born story-teller, but a Jacobs story without
humour is like an egg without salt, or motoring
on a dark night. He is an author with one speciality:
he has the courage or the wisdom to keep to it
(almost always), and I do not suppose that the reading
world will ever tire of the Jacobs brand of humorous
sailormen stories. He and Conrad both deal with
the sea—so differently. Sometimes I wonder what
Conrad thinks of Jacobs, and what Jacobs thinks of
Conrad.

Two encounters with him I remember. They
were pointed meetings. After he had become
successful he asked me if I approved of his intention

to resign from the Civil Service and devote himself entirely to story writing.

" No, no, no," was my emphatic answer.

He did not take my advice. He resigned from the Civil Service.

Some years later he turned to me at some kind of a literary gathering, I forget what, looking prosperous with a new tie, and a well-cut coat, and he said, " You were wrong."

Jacobs' books in the public libraries are well thumbed. The mention of his name brings a smile and a chirrup; everybody has a feeling of gratitude for the entertainment he has given; but it is difficult to remember individual stories or episodes.

I asked an American woman what she thought of W. W. Jacobs.

After a brief reflection, she said : " Oh yes, I know—the humorous Englishman ! He's one of the few funny writers I like."

" Do you specifically recall any of his books ? " I asked.

" No, I don't think so. Oh, yes ; I do remember something about a cargo."

So I began to read to her the first tale in *Many Cargoes*—

" Yes, I've sailed under some 'cute skippers in my time," said the Night Watchman, " but the one I'm going to tell you about ought never to have been trusted out without 'is ma. A good many o' my skippers had fads, but this one . . ."

XXX. LIONEL JOHNSON

POETS seem to consider the term " Minor
Poet " a reproach. I said once to a versifier,
" Who thinks less of a man for being a Minor
Prophet, so why should a maker of verses object
to being called a Minor Poet ? " There is really no
other term.

Lionel Johnson was a minor poet. He was also
an extremely fastidious and scholarly writer of
prose. He was a critic, a very fine critic. He lived
by criticism, but it was poetry that he loved.

I knew him for many years. I will not say I knew
him well, for I do not think that anyone knew this
slight, refined, cloistral man well. After a successful career at Winchester School, and New College,
Oxford, he took chambers in Clifford's Inn, at the
corner of Fleet Street and Chancery Lane, but
hidden from passers-by. There he lived alone with
his books, often " sporting his oak," that is, locking
the door against visitors. Once the porter said
to a caller, " He've been in there two days without
seeing nobody. I don't like it." When Johnson
was in his monastic retirement it was impossible
to draw him out, or induce him to answer letters
or telegrams. Many a time, when I was editing
The Academy, have I sent messengers to Clifford's
Inn to beg Lionel Johnson to deliver the article
that he had promised by a certain date. No reply.

A week later, perhaps, he would enter the office with the review. He never troubled to find an excuse for his remissness : he would steal gently into the room, hand the copy to me, smiling his strange, interior smile, so gentle and quizzical, yet so radiant, so knowing, yet so wistful; then he would relapse into silence, and roam round the room, picking books from the shelves, and smiling at passages. I would watch him furtively, for his ascetic, sensitive, boyish face carried a world of meaning. When William Butler Yeats said that Lionel Johnson's silences had beak and claw, he said precisely the right thing.

But he was far from being an uncommunicative man. He had many friends, at least he liked to say that he had many friends, and he loved to dedicate individual poems to these friends. Although tolerably silent in company, he was always within the aura of the conversation. He was sympathetic, there was not a touch of arrogance in his composition, but I always felt that wherever he was, or whatever he was doing, he was living an interior life. He had insight as well as sight, in Plato's phrase. Once he asked the editorial staff of *The Academy* to spend an evening with him at Clifford's Inn. It was the neatest and the most scholarly chamber that I have ever seen. He was a charming host, so modest and quiet that he seemed to be like a guest in his own house. We did the talking. His method of entertaining us consisted in moving silently from bookshelf to bookshelf, picking a volume that had some particular interest, an autograph letter or marginal notes by the author, and showing it to us with a proud smile and the air of a man who is displaying a Limoges enamel or a priceless miniature.

When he came down from Oxford he began to write for *The Academy* and continued under various editors. He was a contributor to cultivate and nurse, for his reviews were exceptional. They were essays, scholarly, reticently rhetorical, and expressed in beautiful prose. I felt that an issue of *The Academy* without a review by Lionel Johnson left a blank in the paper. So gently magnificent were some of his phrases that we would declaim them aloud, when reading the proofs, for the mere pleasure of hearing the harmonies of his sonorous and sensitive periods. I remember one of the passages to this day, " Some dim half-murmured thought of Pascal, some deep and plangent utterance of Lucretius."

So I was somewhat disappointed on reading *Reviews and Critical Papers*, by Lionel Johnson, collected by Robert Shafer from back numbers of *The Academy*, to find that he has only included the articles that were signed by Lionel Johnson, and has omitted altogether the anonymous papers from his pen. They were, in my opinion, far finer than the signed articles, because I allowed him to choose his own subjects. I never gave him a book for review without first intruding into his silence, and finding out if he would like to write on that particular author.

These signed articles contain reviews of *The Light that Failed, Life's Handicap*, and *Barrack Room Ballads*, by Kipling ; *The Wrecker*, by R. L. Stevenson and Osbourne ; *Ballads and Songs*, by John

N

Davidson; *One of our Conquerors*, by George Meredith, and *The Religion of a Literary Man*, by Richard Le Gallienne. The last named might be taken as an example, in a School of Journalism, of the way a review should be written. The subject matter of the book must have been intensely antipathetic to Lionel Johnson, but he shows no sign of animosity. He is perfectly fair and just, makes no attempt to prove that Le Gallienne is wrong, but devotes all his learning and sympathy to explaining the author's purpose and meaning, although all through the review the wary reader can feel Lionel Johnson's sad, silent smile of disapproval.

His poems have been collected, and are now in their final form. To many their religious bias is too strong for congenial reading, but there are some that haunt the reader, and express the innermost sanctuary of this lonely, unhappy-happy, chivalrous man.

Is he becoming popular? I find, in *John O'London's Weekly*, half a page of " Nibbles from Lionel Johnson." That title would have amused him. Here is one of the " Nibbles " showing his great tolerance : " No one is intolerably and divinely right, no one pathetically and stubbornly wrong."

Here is another : " Of modern writers, only Mr. Pater shares with Mr. Stevenson this fine anxiety not to play life false by using inaccurate expressions."

He owed much to Walter Pater. Always he was his devoted disciple. One of his last contributions to *The Academy* was a threnody on Walter Pater, brimming with love and fealty. Another beautiful poem is " By the Statue of King Charles," a subject near to his heart. It has been published as a broadside, with a cut from a contemporary print.

How much of Lionel Johnson will live? Certainly his *Art of Thomas Hardy*, perhaps the profoundest and most sympathetic study of a contemporary novelist of genius ever written. Also a few of his poems. He was not a creative writer. He was a fastidious and chivalrous commentator and interpreter, always seeing the finest in what he judged. He called himself "Poet and Critic." That expresses him.

XXXI. STEPHEN LEACOCK

EVERYTHING was arranged for my article on Stephen Leacock, "University Professor and Humorist." All was neatly prepared, and I was " on time." I had planned to begin the article at ten in the morning. The clock struck ten as I took up my pen, and surveyed the little pile of newspaper cuttings about Leacock—essays, interviews, comments—most of them dealing with his visit to London as lecturer. And there were my own notes : (1) Why is he so popular ? (2) Why did the London press give him such an ovation ? (3) Recall what you have read of his books. (4) Do you laugh much at his writings ? (5) Describe his speech at the Lotus Club, New York. (6) Describe his first lecture in London with the editor of *Punch* in the chair. (Question, was the laughter of the editor of *Punch* genuine ?) (7) Briefly sketch his life. (8) Is there on record another case of a Political Economist who was humorous ? (9) Have you ever known anybody who laughed aloud at his " Boarding-house Geometry " ? (10) Sum him up. Try to be funny yourself.

You perceive that everything was in train. I had even written the first line of my article, " Stephen Leacock has told the world that he would sooner have written *Alice in Wonderland* than the whole *Encyclopedia Britannica*." I was about to begin the second line, when I started and threw down my pen. " Oh, and ah," I cried, " I've forgotten all about that parcel of books. . . ." It was then three minutes past ten.

I hurried to the Unopened Parcels department of my study and dragged out a fat package. It was labelled " Books by Stephen Leacock "; it came into my possession thus. Some weeks ago I remarked to a member of the John Lane firm (they publish Leacock's books) that I was about to write upon him, and said that I would like to look at the illustrated edition of *Nonsense Novels*. " By all means," replied the John Lane partner, " I'll have a parcel of his books made up for you " (publishers are extraordinarily kind). . . . I had forgotten all about the parcel. Eagerly I cut the string and arranged the books, there were twelve of them, into two symmetrical piles. All except two, which are serious, have gay pictures in colour on the jackets by A. H. Fish. Here are the two piles.

Mostly Funny :—

Literary Lapses, Nonsense Novels, Sunshine Sketches, Behind the Beyond, Arcadian Adventures, Moonbeams from the Larger Lunacy, Further Foolishness, Frenzied Fiction, Winsome Winnie, The Hohenzollerns in America.

Fairly Serious :—

Essays and Literary Studies, The Unsolved Riddle of Social Justice.

It was then seventeen minutes past ten.

I am careful to note the time, because, as you

may have perhaps guessed, I spent the rest of the day before the fire reading, skimming and remembering those twelve Leacock books. I read them at intervals until ten o'clock that night. Please do not pity me. I enjoyed those hours, and although I am aware that this gulping of fun is not the way to treat a humorist, he stood the test remarkably well. I did not enjoy every page, for a professional humorist cannot help being professional, and Mr. Leacock is rugged, and boisterous, and determined to get every ounce of fun out of literature and life; but he certainly has the humorous mentality and point of view. Some of the books I had met before, as American hostesses have a pleasant way of leaving a Leacock volume or two in the guest bedroom, hoping thus to insure a cheerful appearance of the guest at breakfast. It was my duty to read these books, and it was also a pleasure. I repeat that thus to gulp a humorist is not the right way to treat him. As I read I tucked pieces of paper between the pages of sections that had moved me to laughter or to admiration of their skill in the production of humour. For Mr. Leacock's humour does not ripple up like Charles Lamb's or Andrew Lang's or W. W. Jacobs': it jumps at you; it hits you; it seems to be saying, "If you don't think this funny—well, don't." I find that I have put pieces of paper between the pages of *My Financial Career*, *The Man in Asbestos*, *Passionate Paragraphs*, *Humour As I See It*, *Winsome Winnie*. But I have not put pieces of paper in either of the two serious books, not because they are not good, but because when I am on the track of humour I like to keep on the track.

The two still more serious books with which he began his literary career I have not read, and probably never shall. They are called, *Elements of Political Science*, and *Baldwin and La Fontaine*, in the " Makers of Canada Series."

As preface to *Sunshine Sketches of a Little Town*, I find six pages of autobiography, dated 1912, McGill University, which suits my purpose admirably. He was born at Swanmoor, Hants, England. In 1876 his parents migrated to Canada, his father settling on a farm near Lake Simcoe, in Ontario. Stephen was graduated from the University of Toronto in 1891 ; he taught school, and in 1899 went to the University of Chicago to study economics and political science. In 1903 he took the degree of Doctor of Philosophy, and now the humorist begins to function. Hear him : " The meaning of this degree is that the recipient of instruction is examined for the last time in his life, and is pronounced completely full. After this no new ideas can be imparted to him." Since that auspicious day he has belonged to the staff of McGill University, first as lecturer in Political Science, and later as head of the department of Economics and Political Science. In this position honoured, but quite unknown to the outside world, he would have remained, had he not published (daring man) *Literary Lapses* in 1910, and *Nonsense Novels* in 1911.

I met him first at a literary luncheon party in 1912. After the repast I said to my host, who was his publisher, " What is the name of the granite-faced, silent man with an interior smile, who sat on your right ? " " That," whispered my host, as if he was telling me an unwilling secret, " was Professor Stephen Leacock, the great Canadian humorist." " Really ! " I said.

The next time we met was at a dinner given by the Lotus Club of New York. Leacock was no longer shy. Success had unharnessed that interior smile, and caused it to bubble continually over his granite face. Success has given him immense confidence. He plays with his audience, or rather we willingly, delightedly play with him. I have never met a humorist who so rejoices in his own humour, and distributes all his whimsical thoughts so bounteously all around. And I have never met so ready a humorist. Here is an example : The guest of honour at that Lotus Club dinner was Sir Philip Gibbs, but some unexpected and important engagement had detained him : he had informed the chairman that he hoped to be with us about a quarter before ten. By half-past nine the programme of speeches had come to an end and Stephen Leacock—this I learned later—was requisitioned to fill up the time till Sir Philip Gibbs should arrive. His speech, which was extempore, was delightful : he kept us rocking with laughter, partly because he was so much amused himself ; and at intervals he broke off, listening like an Indian, or a trapper, for the footfall of Philip Gibbs. He did not arrive, but Leacock went on with his fooling and Further Foolishness till past ten o'clock, and I am sure that he could have continued till midnight. It was a *tour de force* in impromptu humour.

So was his first lecture in London on *Frenzied Fiction*. The chairman, the editor of *Punch*, in his introductory remarks, had said something funny about those who preside over meetings, and when Stephen Leacock rose his face was one expansive smile, so redundant about the regions of the mouth that he tried to hide it with his burly hand. Boisterously he ignored the subject of his lecture, and told us of chairmen he had known, and we laughed, and laughed, and laughed, partly because he himself was so immensely amused. And when, after half an hour, he came to *Frenzied Fiction*, I found that I knew the extracts, but my laughter in reading them was mild and tame compared with my sustained absurd laughter when he recited them.

That is my report of Stephen Leacock. As a lecturer, either by art or by natural simplicity, he conveys his enjoyment of humour to his audiences so vividly, so unconstrainedly that, even against their will, they laugh from his first word to his last.

Constant practice has made him see life in terms of satirical humour. Yet he can be serious, witness his beautiful tribute to Col. John McCrae in *The Times* of London; but I am sure that he meant it when he said that he would rather have written *Alice in Wonderland* than the whole *Encyclopædia Britannica*.

So would I.

XXXII. SINCLAIR LEWIS

IN common with many other people I read *Main Street* when I was in America. It was hardly possible to avoid buying *Main Street* and reading it. This hard, brilliant, reporter-like, intensely observant chronicle of " the town, in our tale, called Gopher Prairie, Minnesota," was vociferously advertised, and widely reviewed. The Columnists played with it again and again. I saw people reading it in trains; and at Christmas time in country houses, I learned to be surprised when it was not lying on a table. A lady remarked to me, " Every American should read *Main Street* as a penance. Gopher Prairie, Minnesota, is the twentieth-century substitute for Concord, Massachusetts! Alas! "

It was no penance to me to read *Main Street*. I enjoyed it all, even the slang; for my interest is acute in the American Small Western Town, fighting its way to success, and taking its culture in hasty gulps. " You can't expect a nation," writes Mr. Sinclair Lewis elsewhere, " that's fighting the wilderness to stop and hitch up its galluses and fuss over a lot of poetry." At the time I did not know what a gallus was. No matter. Many of the words and abbreviations in Small Town vernacular are unfamiliar to me.

I was interested in the story. I was also interested

in Mr. Lewis' method and manner, and quick
staccato style. He writes as if Europe and New
England had never existed, as if George Meredith
and George Eliot, W. D. Howells and Mary Wilkins
had never been. He is one of the new westerners
who are collaring American literature as a full-back
collars the ball in a football game. I do not lament
this rush of stalwarts from the literary west. These
things have to be. The home of my ideals is New
England, but it would be foolish to close the eyes
to the power and vitality that the western writers
are showing. The tale of their successes is growing.
Such writers as Theodore Dreiser, Frank Norris,
and Upton Sinclair seem already an old story :
it is the newer talents that are flinging the analysis,
contrariness, and growth of the Small Town at us
—Sinclair Lewis, Zona Gale, Sherwood Anderson,
Floyd Dell, Waldo Frank, and that admirable writer,
Willa Cather. It will be observed that they use
the novel as a medium in which to record their
crowding impressions of the life they know, rarely
offering a solution, or conveying a moral. They
are too intensely occupied in observing and recording
to pause and consider what may be the meaning
of it all, or to discover the way of happiness—as yet.
One critic, Mr. Jay E. House, rather pleased me
when he wrote, " The trouble with Mr. Sinclair
Lewis is his youth. In ten or fifteen years he will
be able to see both sides of Main Street."

Sociologists, economists, and social welfare people
generally will have to study these western novels.
There is insight in them and observation of facts,
things one does not often find in textbooks or the

heavier kind of magazine sociological articles. After reading *Main Street* I feel that I know something about life in a Western Small Town. I may not want to live there; but it is interesting and profitable to reflect on the eddies and currents, the shoals and prospective deep waters of Main Street, Gopher Prairie, Minnesota, and elsewhere.

For an American writer all roads lead to New York, and many writers, not all, take to the road. So in England all roads lead to London, and New Yorkers and Londoners merely smile when wild youths cry out that Chicago and Manchester are the real literary centres.

Mr. Lewis became a New Yorker. The exactions of being a " best seller " are many, and include writing enthusiastic bits of praise about other authors which are duly and frankly used in advertisements. When Mr. Lewis has time for reflection he can look back upon a strenuous New York career as editor, journalist, writer of short stories and press agent, and beyond all this, close to his heart, I think, nesting there, is the dominant fact that he was born in a Small Town in 1885—the town being Sauk Centre, Minnesota.

He is the author of at least seven books, some stories in *The Saturday Evening Post*, and elsewhere. One of these books, *Hike and the Aeroplane*, was issued in 1912 under his *nom de guerre* of Tom Graham. Three of his books, besides *Main Street*, I have read: *Our Mr. Wrenn*, published in 1914, his first; *Innocents : A Story for Lovers*, 1917, and *Free Air*, 1919. The last named is the best. I delight in this gay, bustling account of a motor ride from Minneapolis to Seattle, and the impact of western "manners" on eastern "culture." *Our Mr. Wrenn* is a study of a Dickens character, with a dash of W. J. Locke, a jolly, high-spirited book, but rather young. *The Innocents* is delightful, the story of a Darby and Joan who meet their fate with a smile, and with pluck.

None of these books could have made Sinclair Lewis a "best seller." They are preparations. He is feeling his way, exploring himself. As I consider them I see a cistern, the Sinclair Lewis cistern with six little taps representing six of his books. He turns on one after the other, producing *Our Mr. Wrenn, Hike and the Aeroplane, Trail of the Hawk, Innocents, The Job, Free Air.* The water flows out in little, modest streams; but the cistern, being connected with a constant supply, is still full. Suddenly he turns on all the six taps at once. Result—*Main Street*.

Will Mr. Sinclair Lewis be displeased if I call him a thinker? By this I mean that besides his imaginative insight which, of course, is his chief asset, he is also a collector of facts which he collates, ponders over and resolves into a philosophy—actual, sprightly and often impressive. This was exemplified in an article by him in *The New York Evening Post* called "The Pioneer Myth." It is scathing. There would have been a terrible outcry had it been written by an Englishman. Here is a passage: "Sam (Sam Clark of Gopher Prairie) illustrates all the Americans who justify—who for a hundred years have justified—by the pioneer myth their unwillingness to ponder anything but bookkeeping and amours."

Here is another passage. It begins with a remark
which is common in Gopher Prairie, " I'm so busy
I have no time for reading."   Mr. Lewis' comment
is, " Time for the movies, auction bridge, motoring,
golf, two-hour luncheons, and exacting perusal
of the funnies in the evening paper they do have,
but being pioneers, they cannot be expected to
observe such inconsequential phenomena as *Ethan
Frome*, *McTeague*, and *The Titan*, such petty events
as *Men and Steel*, *The Dark Mother*, *Poor White*
and *Miss Lulu Bett*."

Yet the author of *Main Street* loves Main Street ;
he believes in her inherent power and her future :
so loving her he chastens her.

Mr. Lewis is a great reader—chiefly of the best
modern novels. He may read other books : it is the
novelists, the intellectual set, that he writes about
and talks about. Apparently he has raced through
and assimilated all the best modern English and
American novels. In his Dedicatory Introduction
to *The Innocents* he said nice things about English
authors, but in his lecture in New York he seemed
determined to make his audience read and admire
the Americans. Although rather long I must quote
his Dedicatory Introduction to *The Innocents*—

" If this were a ponderous work of realism, such
as the author has attempted to write, and will
doubtless essay again, it would be perilous to dedicate
it to the splendid assembly of young British writers,
lest the critics search for Influences and Imitations.
But since this is a flagrant excursion, a tale for people
who still read Dickens and clip out spring poetry
and love old people and children, it may safely

confess the writer's strident admiration for Compton
Mackenzie, Hugh Walpole, Oliver Onions, D. H.
Lawrence, J. D. Beresford, Gilbert Cannan, Patrick
MacGill, and their peers, whose novels are the
histories of our contemporaneous Golden Age.
Nor may these be mentioned without a yet more
enthusiastic tribute to their master and teacher
(he probably abominates being called either a master
or a teacher), H. G. Wells."

.   .   .   .   .   .

Probably I should not have written about Sinclair
Lewis had I not attended his lecture at the New
York Town Hall on " Modern Fiction : an Inter-
pretation of Life." Then he became a real person
to me, a vivid man, with views and enthusiasms,
and humour, and irony, and gusto, who would
rather make his audience laugh than cry, rather
startle than impress them. Yet a serious man—
in the American way, able to utter plain truths
in racy idiom.

When this tall, slim, blond, youngish man
appeared upon the platform I said to myself,
"William J. Locke. He is the American Locke."
The parallel is open to criticism because Locke is
languid and his utterance has a pleasant drawl;
Lewis is quick and his utterance may be likened
to a Gatling-gun. In brief, Locke is an Englishman, Lewis an American.

His lecture has been so widely quoted and com-
mented upon that I refrain from discussing it.
What interested me was that a young American
author-lecturer should be able to draw a large paying

audience in New York, and insist, and insist that the
time had come when American literature must stand
on its own broad feet, and march straightway into
the Promised Land. In asides, and looking back-
ward, now and again, over his shoulder, he threw
some scraps of appreciation at his old friends, the
British authors. But through most of the lecture
he was in the mood of Walt Whitman when he
wrote—

" Clear the way there, Jonathan !
    I love to look on the Stars and Stripes, I hope the fifes will play
        Yankee Doodle."

When the lecture was over, with my customary
enthusiasm, I rushed behind to congratulate Sinclair
Lewis.

" You must give that lecture in London," said I.
" It would go."

He beamed. " I am going to London this
summer," said he.

Has the American literary invasion of England at
last really begun ?

.   .   .   .   .

He came to London. I met him there, and also
in the country, in a half-timbered, Elizabethan
house in an English village, so old, so still, so different
from Gopher Prairie. He was quieter ; and there
was something like a look of wonder in his eyes.
I draw the curtain. I await his next book.

XXXIII. AMY LOWELL

AT an American literary-theatrical gathering in New York I was called upon for a speech. My remarks apparently pleased a dignified lady in the audience, who had been pointed out to me as a patron of the arts, and who held delightful evenings at her house—supper and talk. My speech must have pleased her because, after the gathering, she invited me to her next symposium. There I met Miss Amy Lowell for the first time : the memory of the encounter is still vivid.

It was a large gathering of interesting people. At supper the place next to mine was vacant ; but the talk was so congenial that I forgot the gap until the meal was well advanced ; then the door opened, and a dominant woman entered briskly and bravely. She did not slink to her seat with a muttered apology, which is the usual custom of late guests ; no, she made some bright and quick explanation, seated herself with an air of extreme confidence, and volubly led the conversation into her own channels. To my surprise the guests acquiesced. Clearly she was a person of importance. I set myself to find out who she might be by interjecting gently uttered questions on literature and life into her eloquence. She answered me cursorily, as if I was rather a nuisance ; but she gave me more than half her attention, and a straight-from-the-shoulder reply, when I said something pertinent, and almost witty, about Carl Sandburg. Then I had an inspiration. " Why," I said in my sweetest tones, " I believe you are Amy Lowell." For an instant she glared at me ; then she said, " Who did you think I was ? " A few minutes later I again had the pleasure of arousing this masterful conversationalist to an epigrammatic reply to the following ingenuous question, " Why were you not at the James Russell Lowell centenary celebration ? "

Later we trooped into the next room and talked, Miss Amy Lowell reclining on a couch in our midst, something after the manner of Madame Récamier. She was the centre, the protagonist of the delightful symposium that followed till near midnight, and I frankly admit that she is one of the best talkers, and one of the best brains that I met in America. I said to myself as I walked home, " They tell me that she is a poet. Really, I must read her poems. Better begin with *Can Grande's Castle*, which people —no, exclusive literary circles—are talking about, and which I have heard Miss Amy Lowell is in the habit of reading aloud to admiring but rather bewildered audiences."

But I did not read *Can Grande's Castle* just then. I came across her *Tendencies in Modern American Poetry*, drawn to it by the following statement made by Mr. Clement K. Shorter : " I have no hesitation in insisting that Miss Amy Lowell's *Tendencies in Modern American Poetry* is one of the most striking volumes of criticism that has appeared in recent years." This is a book that any poet or proseman would be proud to have written. It is a temperate, balanced and very sympathetic examination of the New Movement in American poetry on the hypothesis that, " Poets are always the advance guard of literature ; the advance guard of life."

Six poets are chosen for examination : Edwin Arlington Robinson, Robert Frost, Edgar Lee Masters, Carl Sandburg, " H. D.," and John Gould Fletcher. From the poems of each selections are given, but the chief interests of the book are the essays by Miss Lowell that analyze each poet, and what he or she stands for. " Here," I said, " is an author who takes poetry seriously, a student who loves its practice, and understands its message."

In the last essay I found, to my delight, definite statements about the Imagists and Free Verse, subjects that have an absorbing interest—for the few and fit. Learn, obtuse reader, that the Imagists, whose works have appeared in the successive volumes of the annual anthology *Some Imagist Poets*, 1914, 1915, 1916, number six, equally divided between England and America. The English members are Richard Aldington, F. S. Flint, and D. H. Lawrence : the Americans are Amy Lowell, John Gould Fletcher and the lady who writes under the pseudonym of " H. D."—Helen Doolittle, now Mrs. Richard Aldington. Thus Imagist poet married Imagist poet. How right, as right as the not infrequent marriages of London policewomen to London policemen. In this fascinating essay Miss Lowell prints the six tenets to which the Imagist poets have agreed. No. 1 is " To use the language of common speech, but to employ always the exact word, not the nearly-exact, nor the merely decorative word." Also learn, obtuse reader, that *vers libre* is " cadenced verse," that is, " a verse-form based upon cadence "; and, to make an end of this scholastic paragraph, " polyphonic prose " is not a prose form. Polyphonic means " many-voiced, and the form is so called because it makes use of all the voices of poetry, viz. metre, *vers libre*, assonance, alliteration, rhyme and return."

So you see I had begun to treat Miss Amy Lowell, as a creative critic, with great respect, and to learn much from her. My next step in knowledge and admiration was through reading *Modern American Poetry : an Anthology*, by Louis Untermeyer, a book that should be in every library. From the section on Amy Lowell I learnt that she lives in Brookline, Massachusetts,—around her house is a large and lovely garden—that James Russell Lowell was a cousin of her grandfather, that her mother's father was Minister to England, and that her brother, Abbott Lawrence Lowell is president of Harvard University. I also learnt that after many studious European journeys she determined, at the age of twenty-eight, to be a poet, and that for eight years she served a rigorous and solitary apprenticeship, reading the classics of all schools and countries, studying the technique of verse, exercising her verbal power, but never attempting to publish a single line. In 1912 her first volume of poetry, *A Dome of Many-Colored Glass*, was published.

Musing over Miss Lowell's arduous apprenticeship to poetry—those determined eight years of study— there came to memory two lines by Tennyson—

" I do but sing because I must,
And pipe but as the linnets sing."

.   .   .   .   .

A year or so passed, and with the exception of a few fugitive poems by Miss Amy Lowell in anthologies and periodicals I had no real acquaintance with her as poet. Then one of those amazing things happened proving that the wind is tempered to the shorn lamb. I received a letter from the daughter of an American lady living in Kent. I was living in Kent too, at a place called Island Farm, on the other side of the county. The letter begged me to write upon Amy Lowell, and added, " Mother has all her books." Correspondence followed, and it was arranged that I should motor with Belinda, half a day's journey, half across Kent, and borrow those Amy Lowell books. The visit was a beautiful success, and at nightfall we returned to Island Farm with a brown-paper parcel. " What," said my Dark-eyed Niece, " more books, and we're quite out of bacon and sugar." The books were : *A Dome of Many-Colored Glass ; Sword Blades and Poppy Seed ; Men, Women and Ghosts ; Can Grande's Castle ; Pictures of the Floating World* and *Legends*.

Some of the poems I like immensely, such as *Patterns, The Painter on Silk, Preparation*, to name only three ; and I also like this—

" AN ARTIST

" The anchorite, Kisen,
    Composed a thousand poems
    And threw nine hundred and ninety-nine into the river,
    Finding one alone worthy of preservation."

But do you know—what absurd creatures we critics are !—it is the Prefaces that interest me most, the Prefaces wherein Miss Lowell explains what she has attempted to do poetically in each volume.

If I were asked to award a prize for the most accomplished and the most competent Encourager and Student of Poetry, I should certainly award it to Miss Amy Lowell. But a prize for Poetry—oh, what absurd creatures we critics are !

XXXIV. ARTHUR MACHEN

THE caprices of Literary Fame are curious.
Take the case of Arthur Machen.

Casually I have known him for years—
this heavily built man, with the large, genial, yet
brooding, clean-shaven face, a good companion, I
think; but one who keeps many of his thoughts to
himself. We have never corresponded because I
have never known his address : he gives it in *Who's
Who*, as Carmelite House, Tallis Street, because, I
suppose, he is (or was) one of the star writers on
The Evening News, composing articles on anything
and everything that interests his medieval mind.

I have met him at public functions ; at the dinner,
for example, given to the actor-manager, Frank
Benson, when he was created a knight in 1916. I
was there because I wanted to be there. It was a
privilege to be able to testify to my admiration for
Benson's service to Shakespeare. Machen was there
because his variegated career has included member-
ship, for a time, of the Benson Shakespearean
Repertoire Company.

I have met him, too, slouching through the
interminable corridors of *The Evening News* offices,
for I, also, was a writer, signing my name for years,
in that popular London evening newspaper. But
our chief and most entertaining encounter happened
by chance. Rather late on a certain evening I had

called to see a new acquaintance who had chambers in one of the London Inns of Court.

I crossed the quadrangle, dimly lighted; I toiled up the stone staircase (such luxuries as elevators and stationary baths are unknown); peered at the names inscribed on the oak door. After a while it was opened by—Arthur Machen. My friend was not in, but the author of *Hieroglyphics* and I had some good, rapid talk. He is an admirable monologist when in the mood (see *Hieroglyphics*). For some reason or another I have a vivid recollection of that brief encounter—the open door, the snug room beyond, books and a lamp, warmth and stillness, and Arthur Machen standing in the passage—smiling and talking, ready to talk but also ready to go back to his folios.

These memories I have collected because of certain curious literary episodes, relating to Arthur Machen, that interested me when I was in America. The first began with a letter I received from a stranger, Vincent Starrett of Chicago, dated August 3, 1918. My kindly correspondent introduced himself as one who is eagerly interested in the London literary Eighteen-Nineties, and he wrote to me to say that he had just added my " fine feuilleton " (ahem) on that epoch, to his Eighteen-Nineties collection.

His letter proceeded, " My literary god of the period—of many periods, indeed, perhaps any !—is Arthur Machen. You mention him not at all. Mr. Holbrook Jackson dismisses him with one appreciative line, and the rest is—silence. Did not anyone beat a drum or blow a bugle for Machen in those days? Was he then, as now, obscure,

unknown, unappreciated ? Or am I quite mad to
elevate him to a place among the literary ' things ' ?
This last I will not believe ! Largely through my
efforts, I am happy to know, he is beginning to be
read in America—now ; is becoming a ' cult.' But
why has he never received his due, as I see it ?
Can you tell me anything about him in those days
when he wrote his great books—*The Hill of Dreams*
and *The House of Souls* ?

This letter from Mr. Starrett set me thinking.
Had I overlooked a genius, missed a real " literary
thing " ? Had I been so remiss as not to give even
one line to Arthur Machen in my account of the
literary personalities of the Eighteen-Nineties who
had interested me ? At any rate, if I had erred it
was through ignorance.

With determination I recalled Arthur Machen's
" output " as author. Yes, I had read his *The
Great God Pan*, which appeared in " The Keynote
Series." It did not interest me, and I remember
that I agreed with some critic in some important
paper (I have since found his actual words in *The
Observer*) who said, " It is not Mr. Machen's fault
but his misfortune, that one shakes with laughter
rather than with dread over the contemplation of
his psychological bogey."

The Hill of Dreams and his volume of tales " in
the manner of the Renaissance " interested me in
parts, but they did not make me a Machenite any
more than reading James Branch Cabell makes me a
Cabellite. Medievalism, introspection and border-
land imaginations do not enthrall me, unless done
by a Pater, a Shorthouse, or a Stevenson.

Hieroglyphics is a different matter. It was written between 1890 and 1900, but I did not read it until two years ago. I went frisking through it like a colt in a meadow, enjoying every page; then I went back to the beginning and read it all again carefully. If anything could make me a Machenite, it would be this *Hieroglyphics : a Note Upon Ecstasy in Literature*. It is a monologue on literary valuations by a supposed " obscure literary hermit " (A. M. of course) done with sanity, insight, and humour, done at a gallop by this delightful hermit who is always " ready to defend the thesis that, all the arts being glorious, the literary art is the most glorious and wonderful of all."

It was this " literary hermit " who made that fine phrase, which has been much quoted, about great literature being composed in a withdrawal from life, not a participation in life. There are many memorable sayings in *Hieroglyphics*. I shall give myself the pleasure of copying out two.

" If ecstasy be present, then I say there is fine literature, if it be absent, then, in spite of all the cleverness, all the talents, all the workmanship and observation and dexterity you may show me, then, I think we have a product (possibly a very interesting one) which is not fine literature. . . . We have tracked Ecstasy by many strange paths, in divers strange disguises, but I think that now, and only now, we have discovered its full and perfect definition. For Artifice is of Time, but Art is of Eternity."

Hieroglyphics will never be, I fear, a " best seller " ; but, strange to relate, Arthur Machen has written a " best seller." That was *The Bowmen*, a short story, entirely imaginary, that he published in *The Evening News* on September 29, 1914. It has since been republished in a volume with three other legends of the war, and an Introduction by the author explaining how he came to write *The Bowmen*. This tale is still echoing around the world : soldiers, nurses, and others are still maintaining that they actually saw St. George and his Agincourt bowmen intervene, repulse the Germans, and save the British Army. Mr. Machen states and restates his case, that the story was his own invention, but many continue to believe, and will continue to believe, that it really happened.

When I speak, in general company, of Arthur Machen someone always says, " Oh yes, he wrote *The Bowmen* " ; but it is the Machen cult people who interest me—Vincent Starrett, who wrote a long article about him in *Reedy's Mirror*, and has since republished it, with additions, in a little book, an extravagant book, I think ; but Mr. Starrett is pardoned because of his whole-hearted admiration and frank hero-worship. Then there was the professor at a well-known American University who, learning that I could only obtain one of our author's books at my New York Branch Public Library, at once loaned me his Machen collection. Finally, there is the lady who became a Machen enthusiast through reading his Introduction to Arthur Middleton's volume of stories called *The Ghost Ship*. Machen is almost as enthusiastic about Middleton as Starrett is about Machen. I cannot get excited about either. Are my temperate enthusiasms leaving me behind in the literary race ?

Arthur Machen is good at a Preface, and his
humour is of the nice kind that can laugh at himself in retrospection.   Yesterday I bought the new
edition of *The Great God Pan*, for the sake of his
Introduction explaining why and how he wrote it.
Oh, but he is a jolly fellow, for he reprints at the
end all the nasty reviews, including the one that I
quoted above from *The Observer ;* the last one is
from *The Westminster*, which ends " . . . innocuous
from its absurdity."   And then Machen likens himself to a man " who finds a crushed flower or a leaf
in an old book that he has not opened for years "—
and all is well.   It was Beethoven who, when he
found himself in a quandary, gave a hearty laugh in
the bass, and passed on to another theme.

I think Arthur Machen takes himself less seriously
than do his admirers.   Which is well.

.   .   .   .   .

" Arthur Machen," said the lady whom I had
been bidden to take in to dinner, " he wrote *The
Bowmen*, didn't he ?   It's all very well for him to
deny it, but I know a man, who knew an airman,
who knew a soldier who himself saw St. George and
the Bowmen.   And why shouldn't they have inter-
vened ?   Why not ? "

I have yet to read Arthur Machen's latest book,
The Secret Glory.

XXXV. WALTER DE LA MARE

AN author's friends on the press are not always his best friends. Their action toward him is not necessarily the author's fault. It may be entirely the fault of his friends.

For weeks, for months, I read advance paragraphs about Walter de la Mare's romance called *Memoirs of a Midget*. Would he finish it in time for the summer publishing season? could so exacting and conscientious a writer deliver it to his publisher without further revision? must the public wait another six months for Walter de la Mare's " masterpiece " ? And so on, and so on.

Why this excitement about an author, an exclusive, shy author, of whom not one-half of one per cent. of the general public has ever heard? Miss Ethel Dell is known to a thousand, to ten thousand people, where Walter de la Mare is known to one. Why, when *Memoirs of a Midget* was published, was it reviewed immediately in half a dozen papers at great length, and with an abundance of praise, and comparisons with the classics of the world, in this genre, that must have bewildered readers who had never heard of this author? An acquaintance of mine who perused doggedly one of these long, enthusiastic reviews, and who likes to think that he is well in the literary movement, went straight—hotly, hurriedly, shamefacedly—to the Kensington

Public Library and asked for—" Any book you have in by Walter de la Mare." This answer was returned to him, " We have nothing under that name," and the librarian added, " We have *A Practical French Grammar* by De Larmoyer. Is that what you want ? "

The answer to the above questions is simple. Walter de la Mare is a poet, a Georgian poet, indeed Edmund Gosse, himself a poet, remarks that Walter de la Mare " started the rich harvest of the Georgians." The Georgian poets consort together : they admire one another (modern poets have to do this or they would hardly be known outside publishing circles), and so when *Memoirs of a Midget* was published, those poets in the de la Mare set who have the ear of editors, indeed two or three are editors themselves, set to work to write these flattering reviews that fluttered down upon us on " the day of publication."

I do not suggest for an instant that these poet reviewers were doing what they should not do. They admire, I am sure, the work, in verse and prose, of their fellow-poet immensely, and I too am an admirer of Walter de la Mare, but when I saw the avalanche of praise rushing at me I turned aside, and purchased *Memoirs of a Midget*, which is, of course, what the poet reviewers wanted their readers to do.

It is a book of 365 pages of smallish type, and purports to be the analysis of the feelings, thoughts, impressions and attitude toward life, until her twenty-first year or so, of a diminutive person called Miss M. She is small, she is tiny (I wish her dimensions had been given on the title-page), she is a kind of human fairy, and she is quite lovable and fascinating, but there is too much of her for my taste. I confess that I began to skip, for there is a limit to my interest in the innermost feelings of a midget, even when she has quite a Jane Austen-Brontë facility for characterizing the people she meets and making them live. I find that I enjoy this book most when I read a page here and a page there very carefully two or three times, for it is Mr. de la Mare's style, insight, interest in and affection for all little manifestations of nature and humanity that compose his charm.

Here is his poem called "The Scribe"—

> " What lovely things
>   Thy hand hath made :
> The smooth-plumed bird
>   In its emerald shade,
> The seed of the grass,
>   The speck of stone
> Which the wayfaring ant
>   Stirs—and hastes on !
> Though I should sit
>   By some tarn in Thy hills,
> Using its ink
>   As the spirit wills
> To write of Earth's wonders,
>   Its live, willed things,
> Flit would the ages
>   On soundless wings
> Ere unto Z
>   My pen drew nigh ;
> Leviathan told,
>   And the honey-fly ;
> And still would remain
>   My wit to try—

> My worn reeds broken,
> The dark tarn dry,
> All words forgotten—
> Thou, Lord, and I."

I do not suppose that Walter de la Mare will like this article any more than he likes the spreading praises of his poet friends. For he is a retiring man, more at home in a garden than in a club, and it is not his fault that *Memoirs of a Midget* has been boomed.

His first book, published in 1902, was *Songs of Childhood :* he began to be known, to a limited public, as the Poet of Childhood—

> " Child, do you love the flower
> A-shine with colour and dew
> Lighting its transient hour ?
> So I love you."

In the newest Golden Treasury Series, *A Book of English Verse on Infancy and Childhood*, I find two child poems by him. Indeed, he is in all the Anthologies of the day. Most of the Anthologists quote poems from *The Listeners* of 1912, which is, I suppose, his most popular volume.

> " ' Is there anybody there ? ' said the Traveller,
> Knocking on the moonlit door :
> And his horse in the silence champed the grasses
> Of the forest's ferny floor :
> And a bird flew up out of the turret,
> Above the Traveller's head :
> And he smote upon the door a second time ;
> ' Is there anybody there ? ' he said."

But the poem I like best is that called " The Englishman," eighteen stanzas, direct, strange, full of a kind of mystical realism.

" ' England ! ' he whispers soft and harsh,
   ' England ! ' repeated he,
And briar, and rose, and mavis,
   A-singing in yon high tree :

' Ye speak me true, my leetle son,
   So—so, it came to me,
A-drifting landwards on a spar,
   And grey dawn on the sea.

' Ay, ay, I could not be mistook ;
   I knew them leafy trees,
I knew that land so witchery sweet,
   And that old noise of seas.' "

Good poets always write good prose, and Walter de la Mare's prose books have something in them—cadence, rhythm, witchery—that places them somewhere between prose and poetry. They are literary books, but they have an intensity of observation, and a delving into a kind of fairy-land, real, unreal, that takes them quite out of the category of affected literary books. A less affected writer hardly lives, and although Tommy Atkins would not make much of *Henry Brocken* and *The Three Mulla-Mulgars*, there are sensitives who find in these books immense delight.

If what I have written about Walter de la Mare interests you and, if before acquiring his complete works, you feel disposed to sample his method, manner and material, let me recommend a small, inexpensive volume in " The King's Treasuries of Literature," edited by Sir A. T. Quiller-Couch and called *Story and Rhyme : a Selection from the Writings of Walter de la Mare. Chosen by the Author.*

I doubt if a poet has ever before been asked to

P

compile an Anthology, in verse and prose, from his published writings, and when I recall how hard John Davidson, Lionel Johnson, H. D. Lowry, and others found it to obtain a hearing, I am delighted that the Georgian poets have realized the virtue of teamwork. Their praise may sometimes be excessive, but over-praise is better than no praise at all.

Maybe Walter de la Mare is like a learned and retiring scholar of my acquaintance who, when an enthusiastic reviewer praised his *magnum opus* to the skies, remarked, " How very beastly."

XXXVI. CHARLES MARRIOTT

"AND so they came to the Thousand Islands."
Somebody wrote that, somebody who
had cruised among the Thousand Islands
of the St. Lawrence River. I have forgotten who
said it, I have forgotten in what book it was said,
but the line has remained in my memory—" And
so they came to the Thousand Islands." By the
by, there are really 1612 islands. They were counted
when the Treaty of Ghent was being prepared.

It was dawn : we had steamed away from Kingston
on the Canadian side ; we had passed out of Lake
Ontario, and we were now in the St. Lawrence
River, which flows for 940 miles to the ocean. I
returned to my berth, for the wind was chill, watched
the broadening river through the porthole, noted
that the still clouds presaged a windless morning,
and then consulted the map. Soon we should be
among the Thousand Islands ; then we would reach
Prescott, where I had been told by an amiable
seaman that we must change boats, as the large
pleasure steamer, like a great white bird, into which
we were crowded, was too unwieldy to shoot the
rapids. We must exchange into a smaller, blunter,
flatter boat which cared not for the whirlpools, nor
the nine navigable rapids with a total fall of some
209 feet, which we must descend before we make
Montreal about sundown. It was really rather

exciting and adventurous, in anticipation ; a minor adventure, and in thinking about it I thought of Charles Marriott.

Why ?

Well, whenever I go forth upon an adventure a little more spirited than the routine of ordinary life I think of Charles Marriott. He it was who gave me a taste for the wild—finding the way by compass, sleeping in uncomfortable inns, and even seeking in squaggy bogs the source of a river. Together, on a walking tour round Cornwall, we tracked, and found, on a remote moor, the source of the Tamar : that is, he found it. He is more expert in such matters than I. Together we studied the ways and customs of the detached and silent Cornishmen who for centuries were cut off from the rest of England by the River Tamar, and who still call the residents of Devonshire and the rest of England " foreigners." Together we discussed stories about Cornwall and Cornishmen : he writes them.

Charles Marriott is not a Cornishman by birth. He is descended from Flemish refugees, who settled in Essex in the sixteenth century. He, I think, comes from the midlands : after leaving school he spent two years at the National Art Training College, South Kensington, meaning, I suppose, to be an artist. It was not to be. Manifestly his career was literature, but not yet. He dallied with chemistry and photography, did a little drawing and painting, and in his leisure hours wrote a remarkable book.

Well do I remember the interest that *The Column*, his first work, published in 1901, aroused in literary

circles. It was " written." I use this word in the
way one describes a book by Stevenson, Henley or
Quiller-Couch as " written," that is, it was a work
of art—shaped, finished, done with an air, and perhaps more closely related to literature than to life.
It was romantic, not realistic : the characters were
natural, and they behaved naturally ; but they were
the kind of people that, if you do not meet them
every day, you hope some day to meet.

The scene of *The Column* was laid in Cornwall,
and it was this book that first aroused my interest
in the Delectable Duchy, and sent me, year after
year, whenever I could escape from London, to
Cornwall, there to write and paint, to take long
walks, seeking the prehistoric monuments, and to
watch the Atlantic waves beating against the granite
cliffs.

At St. Ives, where Marriott wrote *The Column*,
there was a colony of painters and writers. He
worked in a little house perched on the cliff, and I
think that he must have been very pleased with the
success *The Column* achieved in London.

Sidney Colvin, who had done so much for R. L.
Stevenson, wrote enthusiastically about *The Column*,
and it was chiefly owing to him that this first book
by a new writer was launched into success. A great
future was prophesied for Charles Marriott, and
from his little house on the Cornish cliff he proceeded
to send out into the great world, year after year,
stories, travel books and essays which writers and
literary persons read with delight, but which, I
fear, were somewhat too well-written and too
fastidious for the general public.

To me a new book by Charles Marriott is always a keen intellectual treat. Well do I remember the pleasure that *The House on the Sands, Genevra, Now, The Dewpond, The Unpetitioned Heavens* and *Subsoil* gave me. He never truckled to the groundlings : he proceeded on his austere, sensitive way, and he was one of the few writers who understood art, and who could make an artist think and act like an artist.

His books were mainly about Cornwall. He seemed so definitely an integral part of Cornwall that it was a shock one day to learn that he had been caught by the lure of London, and that he was leaving Cornwall to take up a position as art critic of the *St. James's Gazette*. He continued to write uncommon and delightful novels ; but I had to get used to greeting his alert, pioneer face, not on the trackless moors above Zennor, not on the cliff path that leads from Sennen Cove round by Land's End to Lamorna, but in London picture galleries, and on the sophisticated pavement of Bond Street. But he seemed to be quite happy, and when the war broke out, and he joined the staff of the Censor's Office, which meant long, regular hours and little leisure, he seemed to be happier than ever. One day I asked him why, and he answered, with a smile : " Because now I am in receipt of a regular income."

I found that in his case regular pay was good for literature. He wrote better than ever. An article signed C. M. became an attractive asset to a paper, and it was plain that when he cared to resume regular novel writing accompanied by irregular remuneration he would plough a wider, deeper furrow.

" . . . And so they came to the Thousand Islands." We began to count them; we said— "How lovely! How picturesque!" We pushed into and discommoded each other in the desire to see more islands. But when I had counted up to fifty I retired from the game, sought a chair and a book, from which I was presently roused by the command to change boats preparatory to shooting the first rapids.

We shot them. It was nearly as exciting as crossing Forty-Second Street, New York, on a *matinée* day. Then we stopped at a place called— Cornwall.

What Cornishman, I wonder, gave to this riverside town on the St. Lawrence the name of Cornwall? "Well," I said to myself, "I shall have something to tell Charles Marriott when next we cross the Tamar into Cornwall." And I will tell him, too, that, as we shot rapid after rapid, and saw here and there a solitary figure in a solitary canoe, feeling and finding his way down the river, I thought of "The Canadian Boat Song." How does it go?

> " Row, brothers, row, the stream runs fast,
>   The rapids are near, and the daylight's past."

And of that yearning stanza that has sung itself into the hearts of so many exiles—

> " From the low shieling of the distant island
>   Mountains divide us and a waste of seas,
>   But still our hearts are young, our hearts are Highland,
>   And we in dreams behold the Hebrides."

And shall I suggest to C. M. that, as he has written so prettily and wittily about the Rhine, he should next write about the St. Lawrence, and raise a literary monument to him who founded Cornwall there?

XXXVII. H. B. MARRIOTT-WATSON

MARRIOTT-WATSON was a Romantic. In his books he rarely fingered actual life. For some reason or another the eighteenth century took possession of him, and from studying it he acquired a style vivid, but of extreme artifice. This manufactured style never quite left him. He lived by his pen. He wrote sword and cloak novels with occasional incursions into modern life, but he could not acquire the instinct, the *flair* which Robert Louis Stevenson possessed. Marriott-Watson was second even to Anthony Hope. He was so clever a man that he could master the technique, but he did not seem able to breathe life into his technique.

I knew him well. Indeed, we lived together for two years, and I have often watched his way of working. He would sit in a deep chair for hours, biting his lips, and frowning, planning an article or a chapter; then he would rise, stalk to his desk and write at a rapid rate in his small, thick handwriting. He was a man more than six feet tall, with a great bushy head of hair. Somebody said that he looked like an Assyrian king, but that his hair was neither curled nor scented. His great height seemed to hold him aloof from the give and take of the world; his well-stored brain and quick fancy played continually with the modes and manners of a past day.

He was born in Australia. When a boy he was

taken by his father to New Zealand. In 1885 he visited London with his father, and " decided that London was too good a place to leave." In his own phrase he " took up journalism." That was in 1887. I do not know quite what he meant by " taking up journalism," for he was quite an unlikely journalist. He had no scent for news, and no interest in ephemera. I believe he sent correspondence to Australian papers, but I never heard him mention the word politics, and he was little interested in the matters that concern most journalists. In his own way he was rather other-worldly, interested in stars, visions founded on fact, and daring speculations.

When I first knew him, he was living, or rather he had a study on the ground floor of a house in Mecklenberg Square, Bloomsbury, with an ambition to make a guinea a day by writing. He found it difficult, for his style was not persuasive, and he was interested in thoughts and things that the ordinary reader of newspapers does not trouble himself about. Frederick Greenwood, who was then editing the *St. James's Gazette*, gave him more or less regular work, and it was about this time that his first novel *Marahuna* was accepted, but I do not fancy that it had much success. Marriott-Watson was a fine writer in a queer, stilted, scholarly, up-in-the-clouds way, but he was never popular. Himself the sweetest, gentlest of creatures, never angry, usually amused, he had no sympathy with any kind of violence. Yet he loved to write about gallant " Galloping Dick," highwaymen, ladies with dark eyes and noble natures, and bucks.

One of his earliest London friends was J. M. Barrie.

They wrote a play together on Richard Savage, the poet, which failed. There was nothing of the real Barrie in this youthful drama. I was at the first performance. I have forgotten all about the play, but retain a vivid recollection of these two, then, young authors when they were called before the curtain by their friends—one so tall and shaggy, the other so small and wan. Mutt and Jeff are not in the least like Barrie and Marriott-Watson, but I never see Mutt and Jeff in a picture, standing side by side, but I think of Barrie and Marriott-Watson taking the call after the performance of *Richard Savage*, so shy, so unversed in taking calls.

When the *Scots Observer* was started, Marriott-Watson became one of Henley's young men, and I shall always hold that he did his best work under Henley's influence. For months, indeed I believe for two or three years, he published a weekly article in the *Scots Observer* and *National Observer*. Some of them have since been collected in *Diogenes of London*, and I think in *At the First Corner*. They were exercises in romantic writing, brisk, unreal and fantastic. The general public, I am sure, made nothing of them, but we of the *Scots* and the *National Observer* considered them fine. They quite made Marriott-Watson's name in those inner literary circles where the *Scots* and *National Observer* were regarded as the last word in good writing and straight thinking. I have been reading *Diogenes of London* lately and find that I have quite fallen out of the way of such writing. It has no simplicity, no real intimacy ; it is not life : it is lamp and desk writing, but a powerful writer holds the pen.

When the Honourable Waldorf Astor, as he then was, acquired the *Pall Mall Gazette* and the *Pall Mall Budget*, and started the *Magazine*, Marriott-Watson was appointed assistant-editor of the *Gazette*. He could write on anything, and because he could write on anything his articles on anything lacked conviction ; but they were clever and he was very popular in the office. He and I were living together in St. John's Wood at the time, and the drawback to being on an evening paper was that he was obliged to have his breakfast at half-past six each morning, and journey to the office in a cab, which was at the door punctually at seven. Sometimes I would have breakfast with Marriott, and he was wont to remark, " You are the only man in the world who can be cheerful at a 6.30 a.m. breakfast." Later on he became assistant editor of *Black and White*, the pictorial weekly, that essayed to rival the *Graphic* and the *Illustrated London News*. With his great facility, Marriott-Watson turned easily from articles to pictures.

Some time after this he married "Graham R. Tomson," the poet, and they settled at Sheer in Surrey. He wrote occasional journalistic articles, but most of his time was spent in novel writing, which became a kind of profession to him. I was delighted to read, in one of the notices of his life, this statement : " Many of his books, including *The Skirts of Happy Chance*, *The King's Highway*, *Rosalind in Arden*, and *The House in the Downs*, have a multitude of grateful readers." I was glad to learn this, for I must admit that I have only read two of Marriott-Watson's forty-two novels, his

first, *Marahuna*, and *Galloping Dick*. It seems a
pity that so fine and well-stored and inventive an
intelligence could find no profitable outlet but
fiction. So it is. Is the writing of novels the only
marketable form of literary production that a man
like Marriott-Watson can turn his hand to? I
suppose so. He never talked about what he was
doing, so I have no means of judging whether he
enjoyed producing this long series of romantic books.
Occasionally he tried his hand at a novel of modern
life, as in *The Flower of the Heart*. He was also a
deft hand at the making of short stories, some of
which dealt with his memories of life in New
Zealand.

I am inclined to moralize over his torrent of
forty-two novels. But why? It was his method
of earning a living. His recreations were gardening,
and taking long walks with his dog. I have a happy
recollection of the last time I saw him. Belinda
and I were motoring through Surrey, and I said,
" Let us stop at Sheer and see the Marriott-
Watsons." Hardly were the words uttered when
he appeared, striding down the hillside, his dog at
his heels. He was just the same, just the Marriott
of the old days, and when I asked, " What are you
doing so far from home ? " " Oh," he replied, " I'm
thinking out a plot, I can do it much better when
walking." We left him striding across the heather
and made our way to his house. His wife was
shelling peas in the garden, and by her side were
sheets of paper and a pencil. I told her that we
had met Marriott walking, but that he was really
thinking out a plot. " Yes," she replied. " And I

am ostensibly shelling peas, but I'm really making a poem," and she pointed to the sheets of paper, lying on the daisies, a little blown about by the breeze.

Those are my pictorial memories of these two. He, striding across the heather, thinking out a plot : she sitting in her garden shelling peas, and composing a poem.

XXXVIII. HERMAN MELVILLE

THERE may be fifty, there may be five hundred, literary folk who, during the past two or three years, have experienced a literary thrill, a rich discovery in their first reading of Herman Melville. I am one of them. Why I should not have read him before I do not know. Oh, yes, I do! The reason is that I had not heard of him.

He came to my knowledge first through a long article in the *Dublin Review* on Herman Melville, by Miss Viola Meynell. I read it with astonishment and delight, for I love enthusiasm. Writing of *Moby Dick*, Miss Meynell said, " Herman Melville has here endowed human nature with writing that I believe to be absolutely unsurpassed. To read it and absorb it is the crown of one's reading life. . . . It is the wildest, farthest kind of genius.". There is much more in the article, equally intense and fervid, in praise of Herman Melville. This was the more remarkable as Melville, as a writer, was a man of rushing action and actual experiences the world over, the very antithesis of Miss Meynell's quiet, cloistral, sensitive writing, akin to Jane Austen, not without humour, but without Jane's constant play of satiric and kindly rippling mirth.

Well, it was my duty and pleasure to discover something about this newly famous American author, who was born in New York City in 1819, of mixed

Dutch and English stock. He went to sea as cabin boy; returning to America he became usher in a school; then to sea again in a whaling vessel. Not liking the conditions he "jumped ship" with a companion, and lived for a time in the vale of Typee in the Marquesan group of islands. Escaping from what was really captivity, after many other adventures, he left the sea and lived on shore in New York, and also near Pittsville, writing the amazing books that now, after long neglect,, are agitating literary circles.

I believe some of them are still unknown, even unpublished. Here is a list that has been compiled by Mr. John Billson, " perhaps the only man in England possessing the whole of his printed works " : *Moby Dick, Typee, Mardi, Omoo, Redburn, White Jacket, Israel Potter* (sometimes published as *The Refugee*), *The Confidence Man, Pierre, Piazza Tales*. And in poetry : *Clarel, Battle Pieces*, and *John Marr*.

Recently I have read for the first time two of his books, *Moby Dick* or *The Whale*, being his adventures on an American whaling boat sailing from Nantucket, and *Typee*, being his adventures in the vale of Typee in the Marquesan Islands. It is almost impossible to describe the rush, gusto, insight and eloquence of these two astonishing books. Melville takes the bit of prose between his teeth and rushes away with it, at such a pace that the reader finds it difficult to keep up with him. His eloquence is extraordinary ; he seems to have no desire but rapturously to express himself, and to scatter his knowledge of everything that pertains to the subjects engrossing him. These are hardly works of fiction; they are descriptions of his own wonderful adventures in the wonderful parts of the world that he visited; of the strange types he met, from a Quaker whaling captain to a savage who knows no tongue but his own. The many characters are touched in with insight and characterization, and with a prolixity that both charms and fatigues the reader. His characters are not the clear-cut individuals that we meet in the pages of our great novelists; they sprawl; they come and go; they are quite credible, but I always know that I am seeing them, not objectively, but through Melville's quick, deep and unresting eyes.

These books have little in them of the "construction" that we have learned from the French in the art of writing. He interrupts his narrative with pages and pages of disquisition on some subject that cuts into the story, or suddenly presents itself to him. Apparently he forgets nothing that he has read, or seen, or heard. After reading *Moby Dick*, which is the name of a gigantic white Leviathan who roams the waters and remains unconquered, we know the entire history of the whale. It is astonishing. Here is a passage taken almost at random—

"To a landsman, no whale, nor any sign of a herring, would have been visible at that moment; nothing but a troubled bit of greenish-white water, and thin scattered puffs of vapour hovering over it, and suffusingly blowing off to leeward, like the confused scud from white rolling billows. The air around suddenly tingled and vibrated, as it were, like the air over intensely heated plates of iron.

Q

Beneath this atmospheric waving and curling, and partially beneath a thin layer of water also, the whales were swimming."

In *Typee* he interpolates a disquisition on the bread-fruit tree which sustains the islanders. This description, extracted from the narrative, would make an important article in any magazine of to-day. Here is a passage from *Typee* that seems to recall legends of the Golden Age—

"With the one solitary exception of striking a light, I scarcely saw any piece of work performed there which caused the sweat to stand upon a single brow. As for digging and delving for a livelihood, the thing is altogether unknown. Nature had planted the bread-fruit and the banana, and in her own good time she brings them to maturity, when the idle savage stretches forth his hand, and satisfies his appetite."

I shall certainly read his other books. On this subject a correspondent, a stranger, who writes to me enthusiastically about *Moby Dick*, adds, "I am told that some of his latest books are almost unreadable, but I have often wondered whether the thoughts contained in them were too advanced for the day in which they were written, whether they would, in consequence, be better appreciated to-day."

It seems that during his lifetime there were some who appreciated Melville's genius. One of them was Nathaniel Hawthorne, and another was James Thomson, the English poet, and in more modern times, R. L. Stevenson and C. W. Stoddard. Writing to Hawthorne, Herman Melville said, "I have come to regard this matter of fame as the most transparent of all vanities. I read Solomon more and more, and every time see deeper, and deeper, and unspeakable meanings in him. I did not think of fame a year ago, as I do now. My development has been all within a few years past."

Fame has certainly come to him now. *Moby Dick* was first published in New York in 1851. In England it was first issued as *The Whale*, in a three-volume expurgated edition in 1871. In "The World's Classics" it was first published in 1920. It is this "World's Classics" edition that we have all been reading. On the cover is this extract from the *Athenæum*, "One of the world's great books."

It was in the *Athenæum* that Augustine Birrell expressed his great admiration for the author of *Moby Dick*. He tells us that he owed his first introduction to Melville to "that exquisite judge of a good book, Sir Alfred Lyall, who was shocked at my ignorance, and most emphatically urged me to read *Omoo* and *Typee* ; but as luck would have it he did not specially dwell upon *Moby Dick*."

The London *Nation* has devoted pages to Herman Melville. One of the most interesting episodes there recorded was the publication of a series of letters written between 1884 and 1888 from Melville, who was then living at East Twenty-Sixth Street, New York, to Mr. James Billson. The reason of these letters is thus explained by Mr. Billson : " Finding much difficulty in discovering the titles of his works, I adopted the simple course of writing direct to the author, and with the help he gave me I was ultimately able to own nearly all his published works."

There was also an interesting brief biography of Herman Melville by Frank Jewett Mather, Jr. in the *Review of New York* for August 9, 1919.

An important life of Herman Melville has recently been published. The author is Prof. R. M. Weaver of the Department of English at Columbia University. The author had access to a considerable body of biographical material—letters, journals, legal documents and unpublished manuscripts—including a sea novel finished in 1891.

Herman Melville has, at last, indeed, come into his kingdom.

XXXIX. ALFRED NOYES

I CALL Alfred Noyes our Ambassador for Poetry. Most poets are lonely, self-centred folk, intimately engaged in expressing themselves. Alfred Noyes seems really to have taken on the delightful duty of explaining and popularizing poetry to the English-speaking world. Again and again have I heard him in America, again and again have I heard him in England, lecture on poetry, explain to embryo poets and others how it should be read aloud, and read his own poems to appreciative audiences. He recites his verses for the simple reason that he loves to compose them and to read them aloud. Because he enjoys this ardour, his audience enjoys it also. He reads with the easiness of a bird singing.

It was encouraging to observe the large audience that filled the Haymarket Theatre when he took the platform on behalf of the Poetry Society. He spoke several of his own poems, and as the way he speaks them is part of his propaganda, I may say a word about it.

He loathes gesture and dramatic manifestations; he holds that poetry should sing itself, and that when one is reciting another poet, one should do no more than try to express the meaning and the music of that poet. Rhythm, he maintains, is not an artificial method of speech. Rhythm enters into and sways speech. The emotion itself should be so deep that it will pass beyond the ordinary sound of prose speech and rise into universal rhythm. I once heard him read Tennyson's " Break, Break, Break." The music of his intonation fitted the music of the poem.

Mr. Noyes is a sane poet. People accustomed to the stagey, long-haired poet are surprised to see a youngish man—clean-shaven, athletic, alert, smiling, standing easily upon the platform, and speaking poems as if he enjoyed it quite as much as two other recreations he affects—rowing and swimming. He seems to know all his poems by heart. The books are before him, but he rarely refers to them ; he just runs on rhythmically, like a brook.

The poems he spoke at the Haymarket Meeting of the Poetry Society were : " The Old Grey Squirrel," " A Song of the Trawlers," " The Companion of a Mile," " An Attempt to Sketch a May Tree," " The Elfin Artist," " The Victory Dance," and a few of his delightful efforts to bring Touchstone to life in modern London, showing that he has humour as well as narrative power, and lyric fervour. Long after the recital was over I found myself repeating—

" At Melford town, at Melford town, at little grey-roofed Melford town,
A long mile from Sudbury, upon the village green . . ."

and—

" As I came home by Sudbury, by little red-roofed Sudbury . . ."

When I speak of Mr. Noyes as an Ambassador for Poetry, I speak by the book. Last season, besides his lectures in London, he visited, on behalf of the Poetry Society, Liverpool, Stoke-on-Trent, Clifton, Bath, and other cities, and from reports that I have read, he seems to be received everywhere with friendliness and fervour. If one could find an artist with the same fervour about painting as Mr. Noyes has about poetry, the condition of painting would improve. He has written many magazine articles, but the production and the propagation of poetry is the object of his days. He has even gone so far as to say that the sonnet may contain all the facts of life that are found in the long novel.

I suppose Mr. Noyes is quite willing that I should call him old-fashioned. Perhaps it would be simpler to say that he is wedded to the classical tradition and dislikes modern developments of Free Verse, and all things masquerading under the name of poetry, that do not scan, and rhyme, and sing themselves. In his latest volume he permits himself this " cheery sneer."

> " Come and see the silly clown that wears a red rose !
> Roses are green now, as everybody knows."

Once a poet, always a poet ; but few moderns are such systematic pursuers of poetry as Alfred Noyes. He was writing it when he came down from Oxford, and he has published volumes regularly since his first success, *The Loom of Years*, 1902, and the *Flower of Old Japan*, a tale in verse that followed it in 1903. Someone has said of him, " He is quickly responsive, his song flows as easily as a thrush's after rain." That is perfectly true, and since that is essential Alfred Noyes, it is foolish to bewail that he has not the intellectual concentration, thought wrought into thought of, say, Alice Meynell. His muse has not changed much. Here is a stanza from his earliest book, *The Loom of Years*—

> " For what had I to do with love
>   Of aught on earth that trod
> When all the stars that wheeled above
>   Shone with the love of God ? "

Here is one from his latest book, *The Elfin Artist and Other Poems*—

> " ' If I could whisper you all I know,'
>   Said the Old Fool in the Wood,
> ' You'd never say that green leaves " grow,"
>   You'd say, " Ah, what a happy mood
> The Master must be in to-day,
>   To think such thoughts,"
> That's what you'd say.' "

Of all his works, the one that I like best, and that I can read again and again, with gusto, is *Tales of the Mermaid Tavern*, wherein the great figures of Shakespeare's time appear, and talk, and sing, and play, and gossip. Well do I remember the joy I had in crooning the Mermaid yarns aloud to myself when they first appeared, serially, in the pages of *Blackwood's Magazine*. Who has not been inspired by the idea of the Merchant Adventurers ? Here is the beginning of a song about them—

> " Marchaunt Adventurers, chaunting at the windlass,
>   Early in the morning, we slipped from Plymouth Sound,
> All for Adventure in the great New Regions,
>   All for Eldorado and to sail the world around.

Sing ! the red of sunrise ripples round the bows again !
Marchaunt Adventurers, O sing, we're outward bound,
All to stuff the sunset in our old black galleon,
All to seek the merchandise that no man ever found."

Here is the beginning of Section Two of the *Tales of the Mermaid Tavern*—

" Some three nights later, thro' the thick brown fog
A link-boy, dropping flakes of crimson fire,
Flared to the door and, through its glowing frame,
Ben Jonson and Kit Marlowe, arm in arm,
Swaggered into the Mermaid Inn."

Would you like a glimpse of Shakespeare ?—

" And, as he leaned to Drayton, droning thus,
I saw a light gleam of celestial mirth
Flit o'er the face of Shakespeare—scarce a smile—
A swift irradiation from within
As of a cloud that softly veils the sun."

And here is the conclusion of this galloping, rollicking, romantic, and sympathetic poem which ends on Raleigh—

" Yet did they sail the seas,
And, dazed with exceeding wonder,
Straight thro' the sunset-glory
Plunge into the dawn :
Leaving their home behind them,
By a road of splendour and thunder,
They came to their home in amazement
Simply by sailing on."

This Ambassador for Poetry divides his time between England and America. In 1913 he gave the Lowell Lectures in America on the " Sea in English Poetry." In 1914 he was elected to the

Professorship of Modern English Literature at Princeton University. Enthusiasm, a real love for making verse, and teaching people how to speak it, keeps him at white heat, and there is also the pleasant reflection that he has sold 100,000 copies of the "Collected Edition" of his poems. Poets need such encouragement.

His latest poem is his best—*The Torch Bearers*, the first volume of a trilogy, which is planned as an Epic of Science.

XL. BARRY PAIN

O F all the writers that I have known Barry Pain is
one of the few who is as humorous in private
life as in his books. His humour is not
invented; he has no recipe for it; it bubbles out
from contact with his environment, whether it be
at a luncheon table, a public meeting, or a casual
encounter. Being a humorist he is also a serious
man with a philosophical bent. Humour is often
but the foam that plays along the waves, urged to
frolic from deep undersea currents. He is also a
poet. One of the best of the war poems was written
by him and published in *The Times* of London in
1914.

Whenever I meet this large-limbed, bearded,
kindly man, he has cronies with him, who listen,
with appreciative delight, to his ready humour. I
delight in it. Others may not think it funny, but
what is humour? Here is an example of Barry
Pain's unpremeditated comment.

At a certain club a group of friends were wont to
meet for luncheon. Barry Pain was usually there.
Parenthetically I may remark that he is rather an
adept at culinary affairs and a connoisseur of the
byways of meals. He has strong views about salads.
One day, at the height of summer, a water-colour
painter came rather late to the luncheon table. He
asked the steward what the dish of the day might

be.   The steward replied, " Cold beef and salad,"
and he added, " Will you make your own salad,
sir ? "   " Yes," replied the water-colour painter,
thinking about something more important than
salads.   Barry Pain was watching him, with that
slow, amused estimating look on his face that is its
chronic aspect.   The water-colour painter took a
tablespoon and poured into it absent-mindedly one
after the other the contents of the cruets.   These
he threw carelessly upon the green-stuff ; still
absent-mindedly he looked round the table for
something else ;   he added mustard and salt, paused,
and seeing that he had not yet taken any red pepper,
added a pinch of that ;   then still absent-mindedly
he glanced around the table for something else.
Barry Pain, who had been watching him with delight
throughout the operation, here said, " Now put
your boots in."

He commenced to write early, and his first efforts
showed that peculiar mixture of humour and fantasy,
with suggestions of " something more," a kind of
rarefied sentiment, that informs all his books.
Classical scholar of Corpus Christi College, Cambridge, he made his initial success on the *Granta*,
the university magazine, at Cambridge.   His first
publication, when he came to London, was called *In
a Canadian Canoe*, published in 1891.   No doubt
many of these sketches and stories had done duty in
the *Granta*.   The book was not a great popular
success, but it made his name.   It was a new note.
I loved it, and for some time had to check myself from trying to write in the manner of the
sketches and stories in *In a Canadian Canoe*.   They

were so fresh, so fanciful, so lively, so humorous, with a curious and unexpected pathos under them all. In spite of the numerous books, many of them in a light vein, some more serious, that he has published since, I should choose *In a Canadian Canoe* as the fullest expression of his original talent.

This volume, which was followed by *Playthings and Parodies*, and *Stories and Interludes* in 1892, gave him the entrée into London literary journalism. He was on the staff of the *Speaker* and the *National Observer*, and he and J. M. Barrie were among the few young men on that distinguished journal who were allowed by W. E. Henley to write just in the way that they wanted to write.

When Jerome K. Jerome started *To-day* and *The Idler*, Barry Pain was one of the group of writers on those journals who were labelled "New Humorists." His was a genial humour; it had nothing of the metallic quality of George Ade or Irvin Cobb in it. It was mellow, and it was often derived from acute observation of London types, such as cabmen, waiters, charwomen. His story called "The Charwoman," grim and relentless, yet full of feeling, made quite a sensation when it was published in the Christmas number of the *Pall Mall Budget*. It was said that the man who could write that should be able to write almost anything. It is one of Barry Pain's oddities that he seems to be always on the eve of writing a great book, and fills in his time producing little books, amusing and suggestive, but not great.

He is an easy parodist. He took to it early.

Playthings and Parodies was one of his first attempts.
It was he who, when Richard le Gallienne published
the *Religion of a Literary Man*, countered with the
Religion of a Cab Driver. He also parodied Laurence
Housman's *An Englishwoman's Love Letters* with
Another Englishwoman's Love Letters. His parody
of Mrs. Asquith's Reminiscences under the title
Marge Askinforit, is remembered with delight by
many readers.

Sometimes he produces a fairly serious volume,
such as *The Octave of Claudius* and *Lindley Kays*.
His latest work at the time of writing is *Going
Home*, a typical example of the mature Barry Pain—
a mixture of realism and fantasy, blended very skil-
fully. One of the characters is a young man, with
wings, who flies by night, and occasionally rests on
the dome of St. Paul's, and a girl whose longing
" was always to return, to go back again, like a
child that is homesick. It would come suddenly to
her, without the spur of beauty to provoke it, when
she was doing some quite ordinary and commonplace
thing. That very morning it came to her as she
tied her shoes. Tears had filled her eyes, and she
had found herself saying aloud, ' Oh, to be there
again ! ' There ? Where ? She did not know.
But from time to time a memory of its peace, deep
and warm, seemed to reach her."

This curious, short and touching *Going Home* has
a beautiful passage in it, which does not permit
itself to be forgotten. The passage is this : " So I
shall see the story you make out of it," says the
artist. To which the girl replies, " If it turns out
to be a story. I don't know yet what it will be, I

want to know the real things—and then make them
lovelier."

Whether Barry Pain writes the great book or not,
this can be said of him, that he wants to know the
real things, and to make them lovelier.

XLI. COVENTRY PATMORE

ONE of the most vital, lively, and characteristic
portraits that John S. Sargent ever painted
is that of Coventry Patmore. It hangs in
the National Portrait Gallery, flanked by Henry
James and Matthew Arnold, and underneath it are
these words : " Poet. Author of *The Angel in the
House, The Unknown Eros ; Rod, Root and Flower,*
etc." Painted in 1894 by John S. Sargent. Presented February, 1897.

In my opinion Coventry Patmore is the hand-
somest poet in this collection of eminent nineteenth-
century writers. I admit that some people would
not agree with me, but there is an air of distinction
and aristocratic alertness about this portrait that
singles it out from all the others. The National
Portrait Gallery is a very popular place, and I often
wonder how many of the crowd who gaze at the
Patmore portrait have ever read *The Angel in the
House* or his volume of Odes, called *The Unknown
Eros,* or *Rod, Root and Flower.* Patmore is not a
popular poet. For one person who reads him,
probably a hundred read Tennyson, but he is in
all the Victorian Anthologies, and almost all quote
the same things : " Departure," " The Toys," " A
Farewell." I know them by heart. This is from
" Departure "—

" And it was like your great and gracious ways
To turn your talk on daily things, my Dear,
Lifting the luminous, pathetic lash
To let the laughter flash,
Whilst I drew near,
Because you spoke so low that I could scarcely hear."

Here is a quatrain called " Courtesy "—

" Love's perfect blossom only blows
Where noble manners veil defect.
Angels may be familiar ; those
Who err, each other must respect."

Years ago I met Coventry Patmore at a house in
London one Sunday afternoon, and was confirmed
in my opinion that great mystical poets are not
jolly companions, and do not come into the " Hail,
fellow, well met " category. We were seated in
the drawing-room, one winter afternoon. The coal
fire had been allowed to dwindle, as our hostess had
been talking in her quiet, aloof way of Shelley, and
when she talked we were unconscious of material
matters. While our thoughts were at their tensest,
Mr. Coventry Patmore was announced, and the tall,
detached, withdrawn-from-the-world figure stalked
into the room. He greeted our hostess with old-
world dignity and reserve ; then he seated himself
in a high-backed, rather uncomfortable chair and
was silent. Suddenly he arose, and said to our
hostess, " If you will permit me, I will go downstairs
and put on my topcoat." Presently he returned,
buttoned up and brooding. He resumed his seat
but did not utter another word. After he had
departed, I said to my hostess, Mrs. Meynell, " I

R

believe the Poet was cold," and the regret and grief that she put into her ejaculation, "Oh!" has remained with me to this day.

Coventry Patmore has five lines in the "Proper Names Volume" of the Century Dictionary—"Born at Woodford, Essex. An English poet and writer. He was assistant librarian at the British Museum 1847 to 1868. He published *Poems* 1844; *Tammerton Church Tower*, etc., 1853; *The Angel in the House*, in four parts, 1854–62, etc."

Among the etc. are two small volumes, *Principle in Art*, and *Religio Poetæ*. I find them companionable and stimulating: they have been my bedside companions for years. All of these essays appeared in journals and magazines, such as the *Fortnightly Review* and the *St. James's Gazette*. In amiable mood Patmore was apt to call himself a Journalist in the way that Herbert Spencer might have called himself a Billiard Player, or Mr. Lloyd George a Hymn Singer. His essays are sometimes truculent: they have over-emphasis and over-statements, but they are always the expression of a sincere and beautiful character, not quite at home in the material progress of the Victorian era. One of the most curious and characteristic of his essays is that called "Dieu et Ma Dame," which ends thus: "We must usually feed for many years upon divine things before God gives us the taste of our food; and even when we have done all, we may not find ourselves among the blessed number of those who are called to the Counsels of Perfection and the fruition of God in this life."

Another of my favourites among his volumes is a

small pamphlet, now out of print, containing essays
on that attractive, peaceful, and leisurely section of
Sussex, of which Winchelsea and Rye are the land-
marks. Once he owned a house in the " Antient
Towne of Winchelsea," and I hold that the articles
he wrote on that historic and beautiful district are
among his most sympathetic and delicately observed
work. In 1900 Basil Champneys published a volume
called *Coventry Patmore : Memoirs and Correspondence*, and Osbert Berdet has recently issued *The
Idea of Coventry Patmore*—" an intellectual rather
than an emotional apprehension of the Patmore
idea."

He has lately again stalked silently before the
public, through the volume called *Courage in Politics
and Other Essays*, 1885 to 1896, which have been
collected by Mr. F. Page. An Appendix contains a
Bibliographical List of Coventry Patmore's Prose
Contribution to Periodical Literature, chiefly to
the *St. James's Gazette*, between 1845 and 1896.

In the volume *Courage in Politics* is included
Patmore's Essay on " Francis Thompson : A New
Poet," from the *Fortnightly Review* of January, 1894,
and Mrs. Meynell's " New Essays," which appeared
in the *Saturday Review* of June, 1896.

Francis Thompson was devoted to Patmore. He
found in him a Guide, Philosopher and Friend.

Here is a passage from Patmore's Essay on Francis
Thompson—

" I feel a personal and sort of proprietary interest
in the metrical qualities of much of Mr. Thompson's
verse. Between the years 1867 and 1877 I was
mainly engaged in endeavouring to draw attention

to the capacities of the iambic tetrameter with
unlimited catalexis, which is commonly called the
' irregular ' ode, though it is really as ' regular ' as
any other English metre, and even much more so, if
its subtle laws are truly considered and obeyed."

When Patmore admired, he admired with all his
heart. Here is the opening of his article on Mrs.
Meynell's " New Essays "—

" Since the publication of Sir Thomas Browne's
Religio Medici, two hundred and fifty years ago,
probably no literary work of equal quality has ever
met with recognition so sudden and complete as
that which has been accorded to the Essays of
Mrs. Meynell."

And here, at the conclusion of the article, is a
characteristic specimen of Patmorean praise. He
singles out for special commendation two of Mrs.
Meynell's essays, that on " Eleonora Duse " and
that on " Japanese Art." After giving the highest
praise to the essay on " Duse," he continues—

" I must simply stake whatever character I may
have for critical discernment on my unsupported
assertion that the other essay, called ' Symmetry
and Incident,' rises far above that ' high-water mark '
and that we must go back to Goethe, Lessing, and
Hegel if we would discover any piece of criticism so
novel, of such far-reaching importance, so moderate,
so simple, so conclusive—in a word, so great."

Appendix I. is a reprint of the letter Coventry
Patmore wrote to the *Saturday Review* in October,
1875, strongly recommending Mrs. Meynell for the
office of Poet Laureate.

There is another book, *A Catalogue of the Library*

of Coventry Patmore. It was purchased in 1921 by
Everard Meynell, and from this alone I could make
an entire intimate article on Coventry Patmore. It
contains a reproduction of the portrait by Sargent,
and an exquisite " Introductory Note " by Mrs.
Meynell, which begins—

" Coventry Patmore was hardly, in the usual sense,
a man of letters, still less a literary man, because—
loving poetry passionately, as he did—he passed
through and beyond letters, beyond the letter of
any poem that he approved. You did not hear
him quote this or that beautiful phrase for its beauty ;
he cited it because it was true, because it bore
witness, or seemed to him to bear witness, to a
truth he had at heart. . . . Patmore corrected dili-
gently, because, like other great poets, he had to
wait for the true word. When the true word
came there was no more question, it was the living
word."

Did space permit I could quote endlessly from this
Catalogue, which contains comments and criticism
by Patmore written in many of his books, together
with letters he received from author friends. But
I must find room for Francis Thompson's description
of Patmore in his " Victorian Ode "—

" Last came a shadow tall, with drooping lid,
  Which yet not hid
  The steel-like flashing of his armèd glance ; . . .
  It seemed as in that quire
  He had not, nor desired, any brother . . .
      Then at a touch
  He turned the heel and sought with shadowy stride
  His station in the dim
  Where the sole-thoughted Dante waited him."

And here is an extract from a letter from Francis Thompson to Patmore—

" You are the only man with whom I can talk at all. With all others it is a matter of playing an intermittent chord or so, as an accompaniment to their talk. . . . Yours is the conversation of a man who has trodden before me the way which for years I trod alone, and often desperate, seeing no guiding parallel among modern poets to my aims and experience."

Edmund Gosse has said of Coventry Patmore that he spent a long life mainly in the contemplation of Literature and of Eternity, but in such imperfect relation to other human beings that he grew to speak a language which to the majority of mankind was almost unintelligible.

True. But at his best he showed a shining simplicity, as in " Departure," " A Farewell," " The Toys," and in certain unforgettable passages of his essays.

There is a passage in Mrs. Meynell's essay on Coventry Patmore that might stand for his whole biography : " He valued his country chiefly for her poets."

XLII. G. W. RUSSELL (A. E.)

A. E. is George William Russell—poet, artist,
editor, agriculturist, economist, essayist,
dreamer. He is an Irish Protestant, an
Ulsterman, and a Publicist; and one of the most
beloved, and the most appreciated of Irishmen.

I asked three people what the letters A. E. signify.
Mr. Nevinson suggested that they came by chance.
"Call me A. E. or anything else you like," said
George W. Russell to some editor who wanted a
signature for an anonymous article.

Mr. Smiles maintained, with a smile, that A. E.
stands for Agricultural Economist.

Then I asked myself; and knowing something of
A. E.'s enthusiasm for an Irish rural civilization to
be realized by agricultural co-operation, I answered,
"A. E. means Agricultural Enthusiast."

Presently I eased my pen and murmured, "Why
did you not ask him during that delightful afternoon
you spent in his Dublin office in 1910?"

Those were the brave days when Sir Hugh Lane
was rushing hither and thither in a fine fury of art
activity gathering in pictures for the Dublin
Municipal Gallery. The collection was almost
complete : it was contained in a fine old Dublin
house, and dear Lane, the most alert and the most
intuitional art connoisseur of the day, was still
hoping that the Dublin Corporation would build

him a proper Gallery for the treasures that he had
given to the City. " Come over with me to-
morrow, and see how they look in their temporary
home," he said to me one evening. " Come, and
we'll visit A. E. and his pictures."

So to Dublin we went. We spent the morning
in the Municipal Art Gallery—such pictures, a
connoisseur's choice of essential and vital works;
and in the afternoon we visited Plunkett House in
Merrion Square, where A. E. has his office, and
where he edits *The Irish Homestead* (I hope it is
published still) and plans and runs the co-operative
system with his " comrade, Sir Horace Plunkett,"
for the betterment of the Irish peasant farmer.

I have never seen such an office. I have never
seen such an editor. The walls of the office are
decorated with pictures by A. E.'s own hand,
dreams of nature and Celtic mythology, vast
frescoes, rather overpowering, rather obscure to
me, for, in spite of the tuition of my Irish friends, I
have never been able to grow enthusiastic about
Deirdre, Usheen and other shadows " in the many-
coloured land of Druid twilights and tunes."

But these shadows are all very real to A. E., as
real as co-operative farming. Perhaps one of these
pictures was the twilight he painted " from love
of some colours and harmonious lines " which he
refers to in his beautiful essay called " Art and
Literature."

And the man himself, the big, shaggy, loosely
built, roughly dressed Editor-Poet, with grey-blue
eyes and a soft voice, how he talked—about Ireland,
and poetry, and mysticism, and farming, and Yeats,

and Lady Gregory, and James Stephens, and Sewmas O'Sullivan who wrote the line—" And hidden rivers were murmuring in the dark," and so won the heart of A. E.

And I, through a flash of memory, was able to touch the heart of A. E. that afternoon. If you want to win a poet at the first meeting quote something that he has written, say it outright to his face : he will blanch, but he will be very pleased. The stanza I quoted was this—

> " In the wet dusk silver sweet,
>   Down the violet-scented ways,
>   As I moved with quiet feet
>   I was met by mighty days."

It is from a poem called " The Memory of Earth." I had read it one day in Cornwall, and it had remained.

A. E.'s *Collected Poems* were issued in 1913, with additions in 1919. I have just been reading the comely volume, and although it hurts me to say it, I have to own that I do not think A. E. is a great poet. He has gifts and accomplishments ; he is sensitive and he has taste ; he is a lover of beauty ; a lover of mankind, he is one of those who walk with God ; but he lacks that something essential, the human lyrical cry that Keats had, that Yeats in lesser degree has.

He is an accomplished poet, very accomplished, and very sincere, but not great. There are, of course, lovely things in his poems such as " Reconciliation," " I begin through the grass once again to be bound to the Lord," and the poem called " On

Behalf of Some Irishmen Not Followers of Tradition"; but I feel that he writes poetry because he likes to produce poetry, not because he must produce poetry.

He is a subtle and sensitive essayist. Like all accomplished poets he writes beautiful prose, and he seems to be able to say things in prose, direct and thought-stirring, that he is not able to communicate through the vehicle of verse. In one of his essays he has been speaking of the way art unconsciously reaches out to archetypes, lifting itself up to walk in the garden of truth. He ends the paragraph thus—

" A man may sit in an arm-chair and travel farther than ever Columbus travelled; and no one can say how far Turner, in his search after light, had not journeyed into the lost Eden, and he himself may have been there most surely at the last when his pictures had become a blaze of incoherent light."

Curiously A. E. expresses himself best in the Prefaces to his volumes. This is not strange, because when a man has finished a book, if he be the right kind of author, he says to himself, " Now I am ready to write on that subject," and in his Prefaces A. E. explains his attitude in writing the book, and, as it were, sums up what he had to say in the book. Thus in the Preface to *Imaginations and Reveries,* a book of essays, he says—

" Birth in Ireland gave me a bias to Irish nationalism, while the spirit which inhabits my body told me the politics of eternity ought to be my only concern, and that all other races equally with my own were children of the Great King."

Do you not love a man who can write like that ?
Would that A. E. had kept always on that high
plane. But recent events in Ireland urged him to
write a contentious and bitter pamphlet on *The
Economics of Ireland and the Policy of the British
Government*. It has an introduction by Francis
Hackett (*sic*). I don't quite know what *sic* means,
but I mean it to mean that when Mr. Francis
Hackett writes on politics he always says something
that I don't like, and that doesn't heal. I have
stuck this pamphlet away on my Useless Shelf. It
doesn't go with A. E.'s other writings. I want from
him the Inner Memory and the Vision Beautiful :
not things like his angry, open letter to Rudyard
Kipling, but such things as :

> " We would no Irish sign efface,
> But yet our lips would gladlier hail
> The firstborn of the Coming Race
> Than the last splendour of the Gael."

And I will give myself the pleasure of copying out
A. E.'s Preface to *The Candle of Vision*, another
volume of his essays. It says all.

" When I am in my room looking upon the walls
I have painted I see there reflections of the personal
life, but when I look through the windows I see a
living nature and landscapes not painted by hands.
So, too, when I meditate I feel in the images and
thoughts which throng about me the reflections of
personality, but there are also windows in the soul
through which can be seen images created not by
human but by the divine imagination. I have
tried according to my capacity to report about the

divine order and to discriminate between that which was self-begotten fantasy and that which came from a higher sphere. These retrospects and meditations are the efforts of an artist and poet to relate his own vision to the vision of the seers and writers of sacred books, and to discover what element of truth lay in those imaginations."

It is such writing as this, combined with his devotion to the betterment of the Irish people, that has made this poet-artist, A. E., one of the most beloved and the most appreciated of Irishmen.

XLIII. CLEMENT SCOTT

THE idea that Clement Scott stood for in the pages of *The Daily Telegraph* through the eighties and nineties in London, is the idea that William Ernest Henley, in the pages of *The National Observer*, scorned. Each was a fighter. They did not fight each other; they fought each other's ideas. I doubt if they ever met; but reflecting on those ardent years in the eighties and nineties in London, these two men stand out as captains. I am a Henley man; he has my affection, loyalty, and admiration, yet here I am writing of Clement Scott. Ah, the years soften and simplify, and prejudices vanish in the will to be just.

As a man of letters, Clement Scott does not enter into any kind of competition with Henley. As a poet Henley is in the anthologies, as a writer he ranks among the best. He was a force: so was Clement Scott. But Clement Scott was merely a sound, all-round man of letters, with a pretty faculty for writing sentimental and patriotic verse. He was also the dramatic critic of *The Daily Telegraph*. Therein was his force, his power. He made that position one of extraordinary influence. No other dramatic critic has ever wielded the power of Clement Scott. Papa Sarcey in the *Figaro* was a finer and more fastidious writer, Jules Lemaître was an intellectual wit delightful to the intelligentsia; William Winter was a power; A. B. Walkley in *The Times*, of London, is a joy, but I read his dramatic articles to enjoy him—the play doesn't matter. Yet none of these caught the big public, as big-hearted, exuberant, sentimental Clement Scott did. The man in the street, also the average sensual man, who loves to be chastised into repentance over his breakfast, adored Clemmy. How Clemmy would have slated and hated Somerset Maugham's *Too Many Husbands*, and how the average sensual man would have agreed with Clemmy, after he had enjoyed the play.

Clement Scott joined the staff of *The Daily Telegraph* in 1872. A " round of suppers " signalized his silver jubilee in 1897. Later came trouble owing to misunderstanding about an article he had written. I thought then, I think now, it was merely a misunderstanding. It resulted in his resignation. He then visited America, wrote for the *New York Herald*, and " impressed the people with the serious tone he adopted about the theatre." This quotation is from a delightful book by Mrs. Clement Scott called *Old Days in Bohemian London*.

First, to understand the power that Clement Scott wielded, it may be well to glance at the condition of London journalism in the eighties and nineties. I do it from memory, not from documents. Journalism went soberly in the eighties. American methods, as we were pleased to call them, had not been adopted. The interview was unknown, or so timid that it looked like a dignified article. The word dignified was popular : personal references

were uncommon because they were not genteel : the
"we" ruled the columns : the word gossip was
never mentioned. I remember my father's frown
when Moy Thomas instituted in *The Daily News* a
Monday morning theatrical news and comment
column. It was written in Blue-Book English :
it was full of laborious statements. "Vulgar," said
my father; "who wants to know what these
people are doing ? "

The backbone of each daily paper was the editorial
page with its columns of leading articles. The
successful leader-writers were those who could
employ ten high-sounding words to state something
which could be explained in two, but a few men of
humour and imagination disregarded this fetish of
wordiness, and were allowed to be themselves.
Andrew Lang was one of them. I took *The Daily
News* because Andrew Lang wrote for it. His
leaders were not signed, but you could pick them
out as you find your sweetheart's face in a crowd.
I always bought *The Daily Telegraph* after an
important first night. Thousands did likewise.
"What does Clemmy say ? " was the current question
of the morning among my friends who were interested in the theatre. We called him Clem or
Clemmy, as we called Mr. Gladstone the G. O. M.,
Mr. Joseph Chamberlain—Jo, and Mr. Labouchère
—Labby. I was unacquainted with actors and
actresses in those days, but knew that "*the* profession," as for some reason or another it was termed, was
always much concerned as to what Clement Scott
would say. Mrs. Scott tells us that Charles Hawtrey
and many others would sit up all night to get the

early edition of *The Daily Telegraph* to see what Clement Scott had said about their new play.

The Daily Telegraph was unique—unbelievably unique. It is a great newspaper to-day, because it has gone very cleverly with the times. The young lions no longer roar vociferously; they have been tamed and brought up to date, but they still need a good deal of space for their rhetoric. The wise and clever proprietors still allow their best lions unlimited space. The lions have won this freedom. Once when Mr. le Sage, the editor, sent a messenger to Clement Scott, asking him to curtail his article as there was a great press of news, Scott replied : " Give my compliments to Mr. le Sage and tell him to go to hell. Tell him I shall write as much as I like."

George August Sala was still a power on *The Daily Telegraph* when Clement Scott was rising into fame. The paper was written, proudly, in Telegraphese. It was said by rivals that over each fireplace these words were inscribed : " Ordinary papers call a spade a spade. We call it an agricultural implement."

Clement Scott asserted himself early. Once Mr. J. M. Levy, one of the first proprietors, reprimanded Clement Scott for writing " effusive gush " about an unknown actor and his play. The actor was Henry Irving, the play was *The Bells*. " After that," says the chronicler, " Mr. Levy gave him his head." I must again quote Mrs. Scott : " Nobody dreamed of speaking to C. S. when he reached *The Daily Telegraph* office after a first night to pour out a boiling column. He'd throw off his Inverness,

then his coat—his gibus had already been disposed
of—and, rolling up his shirt-sleeves as if preparing
for a fight, he started." The boiling column (or
columns) that resulted was merely " effusive stuff "
to Henley and the *National Observer* young men.
If they ever read it they laughed, but *The Daily
Telegraph* readers adored it.

Those readers were the great middle class of
England, sane, sentimental, and entirely inartistic,
who in music liked oratorios and " The Lost Chord,"
in art Sir Frederick Leighton and Alma-Tadema,
and in drama, *East Lynne* and *The Silver King*.
When Clement Scott told them that Ibsen was
obscene they believed him, shouted, and would
probably have stoned the creator of the modern
drama had he walked down Clapham High Street.
Clement Scott's favourite word was wholesome.
Problem plays were unwholesome, so he stormed at
them. He hated *The Second Mrs. Tanqueray*; he
loathed Brieux; in heated periods, boiling with
adjectives, he thundered for " pleasure houses for
the people to enjoy good, wholesome, human plays,
and fine, stirring dramas."

Meanwhile the world went on. More and more
people found in Ibsen an awakener, an uncoverer of
platitudes masking under the name of virtues, a
stimulus toward clearer thought and a cleaner heart.
And more and more Clement Scott shouted against
what he called the " Drama of the Dustbin." He
was fearless and frank—that was why those, who did
not agree with him, liked Clemmy. He poured out
columns of belligerent rhetoric in the columns of
The Daily Telegraph and the proprietors freely gave

s

him his head, for he increased the sale of the paper,
he made the dramatic columns famous, and if what
he wrote was narrow, it was at any rate virile and
virtuous. " Give me pleasure houses for the
people," he reiterated, " give me pleasure houses
for the people to enjoy good, wholesome, human
plays, and fine, stirring dramas." He always
shouted, and Mrs. Clement Scott, who is everything
that a loyal, biographer-widow should be, remarks
naïvely on page 165 : " Clement Scott usually got
the worst of the argument because he shouted."

Oh, how the pitites and galleryites applauded
when Clement Scott entered the stalls on a first
night. He always came early : he took his duties
seriously. Surely never before in the history of the
theatre had a dramatic critic received an ovation.
It did not matter then whether he was right or
wrong; we cheered him because he had made a
great figure for himself in the literary and dramatic
world, and because he had pushed the drama up
into prominence and something like glory.

He played his part gallantly. He did not shrink
into the stalls, like some critics, in his working
clothes and a soft collar. He came in like a king,
with swelling shirt-front and a flower in his button-
hole. Solomon, in all his glory, would have
approved.

But the public, though generous, is fickle. There
came a day when his entry was greeted with Boo-
Boo-Boo—horrid sound ! This honest man—he
was as honest as John Morley or John Burns—had
somehow offended the " Gallery First-Nighters
Club," the " Pitites," and the " Playgoers." Was

it because he had slated a popular favourite, H. V.
Esmond, in an article beginning, " Vaulting ambition ! Vaulting ambition ! " Boo-Boo-Boo—
horrid sound ! At any rate after that Clement Scott
was always given a box (managers dislike disturbance)
in which he hid like a wounded lion in a cave. But
we were artful. We would wait until we perceived
Mrs. Scott's charming coiffure (Eve was curious, too)
hesitating behind the muslin curtains. Then
" Good old Clemmy, stick it," or " Boo-Boo-Boo,"
according to our disposition. A London theatrical
audience was, and is, very much alive and eager.
Sometimes I wish American audiences were not so
shy. Fancy the dramatic critic of the *Toledo
Blade* being greeted with cheers or boos as he takes
his seat in the orchestra stalls.

So Clement Scott passes and remains. I honour
him for his honesty. But freedom is a bigger thing
than a view-point. If Clemmy had had his way I
should have been debarred from the stimulation and
education of Ibsen, Tchekov, Brieux, Gorki, Shaw,
Galsworthy, and others. I should have been con-
demned to sit out the intolerable inanities of *The
Sign of the Cross*, and should have lost the immeasur-
able self-questioning aroused by *The Second Mrs.
Tanqueray* and *Mrs. Warren's Profession*.

XLIV. SIR OWEN SEAMAN

ON the title-page of *Borrowed Plumes* by Sir Owen Seaman, which I obtained from my favourite New York Branch Public Library, I found this written in pencil : " Wit and humour."

Obviously these words are intended to classify the book, which is a collection of prose parodies of eminent authors, and obviously the words were pencilled on the title-page by some careful librarian to describe the volume. Were I one of those nefarious persons who mark books belonging to the public, I should cross out the words " Wit and humour," and write in their place " More wit than humour," or perhaps merely " Wit."

For Sir Owen Seaman, Kt., cr. 1914; M.A.; D.Litt.; ex-Lieut. 2nd Batt. County of London Volunteer Regiment, and Editor of *Punch*, is a Wit—neat, natty and caustic ; but I do not detect in any of his writings signs of humour. Certainly he is not humorous in conversation (that is to say, not with me). I have never heard humour bubble from his lips as it does from the lips of Barry Pain, Jerome, and Pett Ridge ; but he is certainly a witty person in print, a little hard and metallic, but his wit is always to the point, and sometimes it is barbed. Would you like a taste of it before we go farther ? Here are the first two stanzas of " Oral Questions and Written Answers " from the volume called *Salvage*.

" Between the soufflé and the ice,
    When talk was running very small
Like little forage-hunting mice
    Whose patter hardly counts at all—
You asked me, as a thing you vaguely pitied
    (Noting the while another woman's gown)
Whether it bored me, when the world had flitted,
    To stay behind in Town !

I answered briefly, ' No, it don't.'
    My many candid friends agree
That it has never been my wont
    To shine in oral repartee ;
But only give me time and works of reference,
    Those mental aids which Parliament permits,
And I can be a match, with all due deference,
    For ministerial wits."

That is witty and neat, but it has no humour, for
humour means sympathy, and imagine the feelings
of a debutante, or a young matron, immensely proud
to meet the great Editor of *Punch*, and immensely
shy, cudgelling her feather brains for something to
say, and then popping out that silly question :
imagine her feelings when the Editor of *Punch*
flashes at her " No, it don't." Sir Frank Burnand,
a former Editor of *Punch*, and a humorist, would
never have answered like that, even when he was
bored and snappy.

I may be quite wrong in my diagnosis. In the
family circle Sir Owen may be a delightful humorist :
at the weekly Wednesday *Punch* dinners he may
regularly set the table in a roar. Of this I cannot
speak, but when I recall the few occasions of our
meeting, when naturally I gave him openings for
humorous comment, or witty repartee, he did not

rise. One was on the deck of a Channel steamer on a rainy, rough day. I was huddled in a shelter, and my companion, a seafaring man, who was enjoying the discomfort, suddenly paused in his brisk walk up and down the deck, and said to me, " The Editor of *Punch* is in the next shelter." At that I stirred and said to myself, " The Editor of *Punch* can cheer me, if anyone can." So I crept round to the adjoining shelter and cried gaily, " Halloa." The Editor of *Punch* lifted his head from the moist rug, and said, " Horrid, isn't it ? "

The second occasion was at a private view of the Royal Academy. An eddy of the crowd drew us for a moment together, and I, acting up to my favourite motto, which is, " Say it with flowers," remarked, " *Punch* gets better and better each week." To which he replied, " Tell me something new."

The third occasion was a public dinner of the Agenda Club with Sir Owen Seaman in the chair. The Agenda Club, I may remark, was an excellent society which was started " to get things done." It had no politics, and no axes to grind : it was an assembly of men of good intent, the foes of slackness and inefficiency, and Sir Owen Seaman, being such a man, presided. When I made my brief speech, being in what Artemus Ward called " a sirkastic and witherin' " mood, I chaffed mildly the Agenda Club, the secretary and the chairman, for talking a little too much about what they were going to do. When I sat down I glanced at the Editor of *Punch*, thinking that so witty a man would thoroughly approve of my " sirkastic stile," to quote Artemus Ward again. Alas, the Editor of *Punch* did not appreciate my humour. He glowered at me ; he looked almost angry.

Well, we cannot expect a man to be witty under all conditions, and it is easy to recover our admiration for the wit, quick understanding and dexterous rhymes of Owen Seaman by turning to the first inside page of *Punch* whereon is printed, always in the same place, and with unfailing regularity, the set of verses that he has composed on some event or foolishness of the week. He is never at a loss, he is always alert ; and he has a proper appreciation of Calverley.

> " In Calverley's delightful pages
>   I often chortle at the view
> Expressed by that supreme of sages
>   About a certain cockatoo
> Embellished with a regal tuft,
> And suitable for being stuffed."

Periodically these verses are published in little volumes, very pleasant to look through, and none the worse because one has sometimes quite forgotten all about the subjects of his irony.

Owen Seaman is also an expert parodist, and for those who take pleasure in parody, the collection in the volume called *Borrowed Plumes* is entertaining. They are very clever, but I do not think that they are as good as Max Beerbohm's Parodies. Those who have tried to read *Sir John Lubbock* will appreciate the following—

" It is best not to follow two points of the compass at the same time. The pilot that steers both for Scylla and Charybdis is in danger of missing them both (Homer)."

Mrs. Meynell herself might smile at the following parody of one of her sensitive sentences—

" Seen in perspective there is symmetry even in the suburb, futile else. Peckham has this dominant note."

His earliest success was *Horacc at Cambridge*, published in 1894, which originally appeared in the pages of the *Granta*. In the same year he produced the *Ballad of a Bun*, a parody of John Davidson's *Ballad of a Nun*. This delighted London : even I smiled. So successful was it that he proceeded to parody other of the Bodley Head poets, William Watson, Richard Le Gallienne, etc., and friends of Mr. John Lane, the " onlie begetter " of the Bodley Head, began to sympathize with him (friends are like that) on these stings of parody. Mr. John Lane replied by congratulating Owen Seaman on his witty poems, and offering to publish them. This was done : it is that classic, *The Battle of the Bays*.

Owen Seaman is a bright and nimble commentator : his eyes are always on what others are doing : he knows just what he can do, and being a gentleman and a scholar he does it without too much offence. But how wrong was the American reviewer who, in his excitement over *Borrowed Plumes*, wrote, " Why he could not have written all of the works of the authors he parodies it is difficult to see." I wonder that Owen Seaman has not written a funny little poem chaffing that reviewer.

Here am I writing about Owen Seamen and saying hardly anything about *Punch*. When uncles take their small nephews to St. Paul's Cathedral they

try to remember the tag suggesting that those who
desire to see a monument to Sir Christopher Wren
need only look around. So one might say of Sir
Owen Seaman—" Look at *Punch*."

How can I praise *Punch* ? We take it for granted,
like Bank Holidays and the Bank of England. I
have discovered that Americans admire *Punch* and
that Englishmen admire *Life* ; and I remember the
words that once fell from the lips of a Minor Wit.
He said, after studiously comparing the two journals,
—" *Life* needs more punch, and *Punch* needs more
life."

In one of his poems the Editor of *Punch* makes a
young lady (he is rather fond of conversing with
young ladies in print) put his " make-up " under
the microscope of her intuition.

> " She had a trick I could not bear :
>   She tried (I might have known she would)
> To trace beneath my ribald air
>   ' Potentialities for good ' ;
> This was to be her future wifely rôle,
> Namely, to extricate my lurking soul.
>
> .   .   .   .   .   .
>
> Under your thinnish coat of comic art
> Crouches a grave, austere and noble heart."

Is she right ? Perhaps she is.

XLV. HERBERT SPENCER

DID I ever see Herbert Spencer?
I may have. But there is a doubt. Here
is the problem :—

In the middle nineties a friend invited me to a
meeting of a Sociological society in which he was
interested. "The subject," said he, "is 'The
Effect Upon Children of Savage Parents.'" I
demurred, as there were many more interesting
affairs happening in London that afternoon; but
when he added : "Herbert Spencer is coming;
that is, he didn't say he wouldn't come," I consented.
For I had been brought up to revere Thinkers, and
I was eager to see the man who had been described
as having "no heart, and totally consumed by his
extraordinary intellect."

On the platform were a number of patriarchal
gentlemen, with very high foreheads, untidy
whiskers, and old-fashioned clothes. Any of them
might have been Herbert Spencer. Not one of
them ever made a remark to his neighbour; not
one of them ever betrayed enthusiasm or excitement,
and those who addressed the meeting talked as if
they were lecturing a class of inconvenient students.
When they sat down they rested their immense
heads on their hands and stared, involved in thought,
at the back of the Professor in front. I was not
surprised at all this. I did not resent it. For I

was brought up to consider Thinkers exclusive, intense, and indifferent, and I had never imagined a Thinker in any other position than that of profound thought. Carefully I examined the Thinkers upon the platform, trying to determine which was Herbert Spencer. I narrowed the choice down to three, then to two; but I advanced no farther because just then something extraordinary happened.

The proceedings were ending, the venerable chairman was summing up the opinions of the various speakers on the effect of savage parents upon children, all of which opinions, I need hardly say, were derived from books, when suddenly a man rose at the back of the hall and said, impressively and with dignity : " I, too, would speak. I was born of savage parents. I will tell you all what it is like."

I turned quickly. We all did. Imagine my delight : before us stood, in a reach-me-down suit, the hatchet-faced Iroquois of Fenimore Cooper, friend and hero of my boyhood, or it may have been the Last of the Mohicans, calm and imperturbable as ever.

" Sit down, sir," cried the chairman. " I must ask you to resume your seat. You are not in order."

" But," said Eaglefeather, " I am of savage parents born. I tell you about it. What it is like— all, all."

" Please resume your seat, sir. Any person desiring to speak at these meetings must submit his name beforehand and in writing."

A woman called out " Shame "; one of the Thinkers cried " Chair ! Chair ! " But the cry

of shame was taken up. Many left the meeting in
protest. I joined them because the sun was shining,
and so I am unable to state absolutely that I ever
saw Herbert Spencer.

But that episode did not shake my faith in the
genus Thinker or the Great Man of Victorian
England. The ink on the perceptions of boyhood
is indelible, and so the names of Herbert Spencer,
John Stuart Mill and George Henry Lewes will
always symbolize for me beings too deeply engaged
in thought to have time to live. Well do I remember my apprehension when my uncle once read
aloud this question that Herbert Spencer addressed
to the world in his *Autobiography*—" Is it really a
fact that women have better intuitions into character
than men have ? "

When Herbert Spencer went to live at Brighton
(5 Percival Terrace) in 1898, I hastened there in the
hope of seeing him. My mission was unsuccessful ;
but I had the good fortune to meet a man who
assured me that he knew the shopkeeper who sold
Herbert Spencer the cotton wool which he was
accustomed, in society, to insert into his ears when
the conversation did not interest him. Probably
he used the wool in the many boarding-houses he
frequented, for I gather from his *Autobiography* that
this eminent and extraordinary man never had a real
home. He lived *en pension* in various districts in
London. Once he hired a room at 2 Leinster Place—
" to serve me as a study, with the option of taking
an additional room if need be." The servants at
the boarding-house near by were instructed to tell
visitors that " I was not at home."

Oh, and I once met a member of the Athenæum Club who informed me that, on two occasions, he had watched Herbert Spencer playing billiards; and he narrated to me the famous Herbert Spencer billiard story, which I had already heard nine times and had told eleven times. Perhaps you may not have heard it. The author of *Synthetic Philosophy* was once badly beaten at his favourite game of billiards. Immersed in thought he replaced his cue, and then turning to his companion said, " Young man, your proficiency at billiards argues, in my opinion, a singularly ill-spent period of adolescence."

Readers of Herbert Spencer's *Autobiography* are aware that he was not without a kind of solemn humour; but he was so self-centred, so crammed with intellectual vanity, so curious about himself, that he could permit his pen to write such a passage as this : " With me any tendency toward facetiousness is the result of temporary elation : either caused by pleasurable health-giving change, or, more commonly, by meeting old friends. Habitually I observed that, on seeing the Lotts after a long interval, I was apt to give vent to some witticisms during the first hour or two, and then they became rare."

But the philosopher could see a joke. He quotes with approval Huxley's witticism : " Oh, you know Spencer's idea of a tragedy is a deduction killed by a fact." On another occasion Huxley said to him : " Come upstairs; I want to show you something which will delight you—a fact that goes slick through a great generalization."

I admit that I have not read *Synthetic Philosophy*

or *Social Statics*, but " you never can tell," because whenever I have read Herbert Spencer I have been surprised at my interest in him, and gratified to find that I could understand a good deal. His essay on " Education " was almost a white stone in my reading career, his " Facts and Comments " was a cheerful companion for a week; and *The Man Versus the State*, a collection of his essays with critical and interpretative comments by nine eminent Americans, showed me what a hold (apparently) the Spencerian philosophy has upon William Howard Taft, Charles W. Eliot, Elihu Root, Henry Cabot Lodge, David Jayne Hill, Nicholas Murray Butler, Augustus P. Gardner, E. H. Gary and Harlan F. Stone.

I felt quite out in the cold.

Still further out in the cold felt I when, on the occasion of the Herbert Spencer centenary, I read yards and yards of closely reasoned, exhaustive articles, amazingly well-informed on the Spencerian philosophy. I felt terribly uneducated until I reflected that it is the business of editors to know exactly, with the aid of their secretaries, the twelve men in the continent (sometimes there are less than twelve) who are experts on a subject that the accident of a date has made a news event.

While I was reading these learned articles on Spencer I wondered what the average American, "the man in the street," thinks of him. In the course of the next few days I addressed myself on the subject to various people. I said to them— " If I repeat to you words like Lambs, Fire Engines, Ice Cream, The Fourth of July, certain mental pictures float into your mind. Now, what kind of mental picture have you when I say the word— Herbert Spencer ? "

Here are the replies :—

A Bookseller—We have some call for *First Principles*—but not much. The *Essays on Education* are published in " Everyman's Library."

A Governess (to whom I had given a copy of *Education*)—I read a bit, and then I had to comb my hair.

A Painter—When I went to England someone told me that he was the greatest philosopher in the world. No, I don't read him.

A Girl Librarian—Oh, yes, I know *The Faërie Queene* and *The Shepherd's Calendar* quite well.

When I reminded her that those were written by another Spenser she replied, " Of course, how silly of me ! He was in love with George Eliot, wasn't he ? " Whereupon I drew her attention to the *Autobiography*, Vol. I. p. 462, where the philosopher says : " There were reports that I was in love with her, and that we were about to be married. But neither of these reports was true."

A Photographer—I have developed the habit of reading a page of him once a week. His clear, straightforward style has a strong attraction for me. I consider Spencer the greatest analytical intelligence of the Anglo-Saxon race.

An Editor—He said somewhere that the use of superlatives argues dishonesty of mind.

A Hyphenated American—I studied him at Bonn. My interest now is entirely in Chinese philosophy.

A Taxicab Driver—Ask my missis. She's the reader.

When Herbert Spencer was in his teens he was taken by his uncle to an evening party at Bath. The hostess inquired why the grave boy was not waltzing. To which the uncle replied, " No Spencer ever dances."

XLVI. GEORGE W. STEEVENS

OUR first meeting, in the autumn of 1893, was laconic. He came into my room at the *Pall Mall Budget* office (the old building in Northumberland Street), and said, " I'm Steevens."

His manners were always nice. You see I was an editor, but not his editor : he was paying me a call, and as he never posed he presented to my consideration his usual shy, sulky, smiling, diffident, engaging manner.

I said, " Oh," and half offered him a chair. He looked at it ; then round the room ; then at me and remarked : " I thought you were a grave, mature man with a white beard."

I said, " Did you ? "

That is all I remember of the conversation. George was never a great talker ; but he was a good listener. I see his slight figure now, slouching airily, making occasional drawling comments, and smiling. It is his smile I remember, his sunny, interior smile ; and his curly hair, and popularity. Everybody loved him. This is no figure of speech. Of all the men I have known George Warrington Steevens, scholar, journalist, man of letters, and war correspondent, was the best beloved, and the most respected.

He left my room quietly—all his movements were slow and soft—and when he was gone, I paused to consider him. He was then twenty-four ; had been for nearly a year a Fellow of Pembroke College, Oxford, and was about finishing the first period—the scholastic one—of his brief meteoric career. His record of medals, prizes, scholarships and honours at School and University was, I believe, unprecedented. In the memoir W. E. Henley wrote of him he quotes the list of his distinctions. They would fill this page: they began with the Sassoon Entrance Scholarship to the City of London School; among them were the Classical Scholarship at Balliol College, Oxford, in 1887; a First in Honours at the London University matriculation in 1889, ending with First Class in Final Classical School, Oxford, 1892, and his election to a Fellowship of Pembroke College, Oxford, in 1893. He was known as " the Balliol prodigy." Of him it was written : " The mere quantity of his knowledge was astonishing; his command over it was still more so. He had a Napoleonic faculty for instantaneous and complete concentration of his intellectual forces."

Commenting on this Henley says : " That is most true. He was so complete a master of his equipment and his means alike, that, as another school friend has recorded, he wrote his ' Monologues ' with a running pen, and scarce ever a reference to the authorities shelved at his back."

That is so. I watched him writing one of them at midnight, in the rooms he shared with Harold Brown in the Temple. Which it was I forget—Troilus, Xantippe, Brutus, Nero, Cicero, Alcibiades —whichever it was he wrote straight on, talking occasionally as he wrote, never referring to a book, and doing it with the same easy tolerance and apparent indifference with which he wrote of a lion-comique, a debate in the House of Commons, or the scene on Epsom Downs while the Derby was being run.

The transition from his scholastic career to journalism was quick. It came via Cambridge, whither he had gone to edit the *Cambridge Observer*. Oscar Browning detected a new hand—incisive and witty—in that undergraduate journal, sought it out, and recommended G. W. Steevens to Henry Cust, editor of the *Pall Mall Gazette*, which was then just beginning under its new editor, and new proprietor, Mr. W. W. Astor, to startle London.

Steevens was then, as Henley describes him, merely " a type of Young Oxford : a youth with a pince-nez and a soft hat and a turn for Ibsen and Zola and all manner of extremes." He was given a desk in the big editorial room of the *Pall Mall Gazette*, where from eight in the morning till noon, a few brilliant young men produced the leader, the Occasional Notes, and the smarter portions of the paper that were not covered by the news and other departments.

Steevens quickly showed that he could write on anything, usually better than anyone else. He had an intense interest in life, with an extraordinary power of concentration on the matter in hand; and nothing seemed to give him any trouble. With the same apparent ease he would turn out in a morning an exhaustive study of Great Britain's sea power as compared with other nations (his *Naval Policy* was published in 1896) and a couple of Occasional Notes—witty, irreverent, pointed—dealing with some fashion or folly of the day.

Within a month he was the most valuable man in the office, and the most popular. He was true as steel under his languid, lackadaisical, sullen, shy, amused, sympathetic manner. He never talked of himself : he never boasted : whatever he wrote read as if it was being done for the first time ; as if a new tale was being told.

He was sent to report a debate in the House of Commons. His account was so direct, understanding and amusing that the paper received letters by every post asking who was the new writer. He was influenced neither by praise nor blame : his delight was in doing what he had to do as well as he could. It was his way to drop into my room, on the *Pall Mall Budget* side of the corridor, when the *Gazette* had gone to press, and once I said to him : " George, what would you best like to do in life, if you were given the opportunity ? "

He answered, " Just to go on as we're going now."

That was not to be. An upheaval was looming ahead. In 1895, by one of those dramatic changes, common in journalism, Henry Cust went out from the *Pall Mall Gazette* and others came in. George Steevens, by this time, was writing regularly for *The National Observer*, for *Blackwood's Magazine* and the *New Review*—such articles as " Mr. Balfour's Philosophy," and " From the New Gibbon " : his pen was eagerly sought by other editors : he stood forth as showing that high classical attainments and a full mind are no bar to great success in the burr and tumble of journalism. But all Oxford dons are not like G. W. Steevens.

There was one editor, the cleverest editor-

proprietor, and business journalist of the day, who
had watched his career, and who, when he was free,
seized him, made him his chief writer, and became
his friend, as everyone else did. That was Alfred
Harmsworth.

In 1896 *The Daily Mail* was founded : in 1897
George W. Steevens joined the staff as star descrip-
tive writer and war correspondent, and I believe
that the success of that journal was due in a great
measure to Steevens. That was his third period :
then it was that he truly found himself. His
articles appeared on the editorial page : those crisp,
bright essays, telling without superfluous words, with
understanding and with humour, just what that alert
brain and responsive heart saw and felt, were a new
thing in journalism. There has been none since like
him. I read his articles day by day in *The Daily
Mail*, and I have gone through them since in
book form—*With the Conquering Turk, Egypt in
1898, With Kitchener to Khartum, The Tragedy of
Dreyfus, In India, The Land of the Dollar, Glimpses
of Three Nations, From Capetown to Ladysmith*—and
I can only say once again that no one I know has
equalled his vivid restraint, and power of grasping a
new movement or a new country (new to him) and
telling us about it freshly, vigorously, weightily yet
lightly.

Read his chapters on Kitchener, on the Kaiser, on
Dreyfus and on Bryan. And read the last words he
wrote when besieged in Ladysmith in 1900. He was
thirty-one years of age when he passed away in that
lonely, harassed South African town, thinking of a
little grey island in the North Sea where his heart was,

of an old house, surrounded by an old wall, whither he would hasten when he returned from his far and many journeyings.

That old house, surrounded by an old wall, was Merton Abbey, near Wimbledon where, in former days, Nelson lived. That was his home after he had married Mrs. Rogerson. Thither we, his friends, would troop when the word went round that George was back; and there we would find him on the lawn on Sunday afternoons, unchanged in all the essentials that made George Warrington Steevens what he was.

" To realize George Steevens," said Henley, " you must put away everything but simplicity, kindness, sincerity."

Much has happened since then—the Great War among other things—but to me the memory of George Steevens is fresh and untarnished, and I say of him, as I said of Henry Cust, his chief, editor— *Viva adhuc et desiderio pulcriora*—Living still, and the more beautiful because of our longing.

XLVII. J. M. SYNGE

OFTEN have I promised myself to write about John M. Synge (1871–1909)—that rugged, lonely, black-visaged, silent Irishman, who cared nothing about politics, only for life, real life, the life of the imagination, and the life of his people of Aran and Wicklow, their dreams, tales, legends and ways.

To Synge the word genius can be rightly applied.

I delayed writing about him until I could go carefully through the four volumes of his *Collected Works*—his six plays, one unfinished; his poems, and translations from Petrarch; his books on the Aran Islands, and the Vagrants of Wicklow, and all that has been written about him by such close friends and admirers as Lady Gregory, W. B. Yeats and John Masefield.

The legend of Synge is complete. His work and life are rounded off, recorded. He stands out as an example to all authors : his brief life proclaims that to write vitally an imaginative writer must go, not to books, but to the source, to nature, to human nature.

Synge obtained all his material from living with the peasants of the Aran islands, and Wicklow. He talked with them, he listened to their tales, such tales, such wild, wan and weird beliefs, so superstitious, so beyond credibility to the sophisticated dweller in cities who could hardly believe them, their pathos and rampant humour, had not other Irish writers, notably Lady Gregory, also heard them and written them down. But these tales passed through the purifying fire of Synge's imagination, and came out gold (so Shakespeare worked), shaped and fashioned into the quick, yeasty, mysterious dialogue of his plays. Turn to any of them—to *In the Shadow of the Glen, Riders to the Sea, The Well of the Saints, The Tinker's Wedding, The Playboy of the Western World, Deirdre of the Sorrows*—turn to any page of these plays, and you are startled by the even freshness, originality, and idiomatic flavour of the dialogue on each and every page.

Synge's life may be divided into two parts—before he met W. B. Yeats in Paris in 1899, and after. It was Yeats who, with the instinct and intuition of a true poet, told Synge in Paris that he was sailing on the wrong tack; that he should flee from foreign culture, fine and filling though it might be; that he should return to Ireland, recapture the Irish view-point and dream that he had held as a youth; that he should aim " to express a life that has never found expression," and write plays for the Irish Literary Theatre, which Yeats was then meditating. The mystic has a practical side. Yeats' instinct that Synge was the dramatist (even if some of the Irish objected to him) for the Irish Literary Theatre was abundantly fulfilled. Synge obeyed. He returned to Ireland, and went year after year to Aran—to Inishmaan and Aranmor, " the islets that are separated from Connemara by racing seas." There he garnered material for his plays and books.

But I do not think that the studious, aloof, sufficient-unto-himself Synge was unhappy in the Before period. Born near Dublin of an old Wicklow family, he was educated at Trinity College, Dublin; learnt the piano, flute and violin; thought about becoming a musician; went to Germany; tramped the Continent on " forty pounds a year," so runs the phrase; read hard, perused books in six languages, Hebrew, Irish, German, Italian, French, and English (so says John Masefield), made a deep study of Racine, his favourite author, and was dipping deeper and deeper into European culture when W. B. Yeats found him that day in Paris in 1899, and switched him off to Ireland. Which was good for Synge and good for the world.

I saw him once—a brief glimpse. It was when the Abbey Theatre Company visited London, in the early summer of 1907, and gave performances, among other plays, of Synge's *Riders to the Sea* and *The Playboy of the Western World.* Throughout one of the acts, in the darkened house, Yeats and Synge stood in front of the stage box (the house was full) watching the performance. They never spoke to each other. They were the quietest couple in the theatre. I suppose by that time they had said all they had to say to each other about Celtic glamour, and Deirdre, and Cuchulain, and Fion, and Yeats, and Synge, and the United Irish-American Societies of New York, and the cheapest way of getting to the Aran Islands from Bloomsbury.

I saw Synge that afternoon just as he looks in the

frontispiece to John Masefield's *A Few Personal
Recollections of John M. Synge*, the shock of thick
black hair, the heavy black moustache, and the dark,
grave face, gravely scrutinizing the darkened house
and the bare stage where the Playboy was dancing
to the Synge wild tune. Later I was to read what
Yeats said about him in *The Cutting of an Agate*:
" He was a solitary, undemonstrative man, never
asking pity, nor complaining, nor seeking sympathy,
but in this book's (*Deirdre of the Sorrows*) momentary
cries : all folded up in brooding intellect, knowing
nothing of new books and newspapers, reading the
great masters alone ; and he was but the more hated
because he gave his country what it needed, an
unmoved mind. . . . In Ireland he loved only
what was wild in its people, and in ' the grey and
wintry sides of many glens.' . . . He loved all
that has edge, all that is salt in the mouth, all that
is rough to the hand. . . . He had no life outside
his imagination, little interest in anything that was
not its chosen subject. He hardly seemed aware of
the existence of other writers. . . . He was a
drifting silent man, full of hidden passion, and loved
wild islands because there, set out in the light of
day, he saw what lay hidden in himself."

It is impossible to describe, to those who have
not seen one, the effect of a Synge play. I understand the language, but I am watching scenes,
hearing talk, listening to vagaries that seem to
belong to another people—and to another age ;
and it all passes to an accompaniment of violence,
and tenderness, and superstition, and insight, and
unnatural humour, and unexpected wisdom : and

all is said in the racy idiom that is never absent from
Synge.

The hostile reception given to *The Playboy of the
Western World* by the Irish in Dublin, New York
and elsewhere hurt Synge. In London it was
listened to with rapt attention, and greeted with
loud applause. Why should the Irish object?
Lord Dundreary did not anger practical England,
Sentimental Tommy did not outrage dour Scotland.
Of *The Playboy of the Western World* Synge wrote,
" Anybody who has lived in real intimacy with the
Irish peasantry will know that the wildest sayings in
this play are tame indeed compared with the fancies
one may hear at any little hillside cottage of Geesala,
or Carraroe, or Dingle Bay."

It is interesting to contrast Synge's book on *The
Aran Islands* with Gissing's *By the Ionian Sea*—
Gissing stretching his longing gaze toward the past,
Synge interested only, and fiercely, in the people of
the present. In *The Aran Islands* may be found the
material he used so wonderfully in his plays—" Pat
has told me a story of the goose that lays the golden
eggs." This was one of the " hearth " tales. An
Irishwoman said to Lady Gregory, " My old nurse
has been reading *The Shadow of the Glen*, but she
says it is but a hearth tale ; she had heard it long ago
in Ireland."

His few poems are rugged and real. There is one
that he calls Prelude.

" Still south I went and west and south again,
    Through Wicklow from the morning till the night,
And far from cities, and the sights of men,
    Lived with the sunshine and the moon's delight.

I knew the stars, the flowers, and the birds,
The grey and wintry sides of many glens,
And did but half remember human words,
In converse with the mountains, moors and fens."

He took no interest in politics, he showed no concern with people in the mass, but he was " wise in judging individual men." And he said once to Yeats, " We must unite asceticism, stoicism, ecstasy ; two of these have often come together, but not all three."

I think that they came together—often—in John M. Synge.

XLVIII. SIR RABINDRANATH TAGORE

SIR RABINDRANATH TAGORE is an author about whom I have not quite made up my mind. As a politician, frankly, I do not like him.

He is, and has been for years, in England and America, a picturesque figure, passing softly through cities counselling Quietism and interpreting India, the India that we know through Max Müller's *Six Systems of Indian Philosophy*, through a poem or two by Emerson, especially "Brahma," through Matthew Arnold's "Obermann Once More," and through Kipling in *Kim*, of course, and in that wonder-story, *The Miracle of Puran Bhagat*. A London hostess gave days of diplomacy trying to bring Kipling and Tagore together at her dinner-table. She failed. Kipling and Tagore have the wisdom of the wise. And there are editors who, in the dream lists of a perfect issue, that they sometimes compile, include an article by Kipling on Tagore, and one by Tagore on Kipling.

He is not an author, I think, that casual readers peruse steadfastly: they are content with remembering a passage or two of the "Things Felt," or "Things Perceived," or "Things Half-Realized," that are collected in his *Gitanjali* or *Song Offerings*, which won the Nobel prize in 1913. *Stray Birds* is another collection of Tagoreisms. By the by, he has at least one disciple who peruses him steadfastly, for in the public library copy of *Stray Birds*, which I have been looking through, I find that a reader has inscribed on the first page, " Read this slowly to appreciate " ; and on the last page he has written— " Read over again to appreciate." This annoying and iniquitous person has also ticked with a pencil the Tagore prose poems that he especially likes. One to which he has given an extra thick tick of approval is this : " The prelude of the night is commenced in the music of the sunset, in its solemn hymn to the ineffable dark." I submit that the man or woman who ticked this is a duffer. There is nothing in it. But he ticks another which is fine, and thought-starting : " Men are cruel, but man is kind."

It is but fair to remark that these Tagore prose poems have been translated by him, or by others, from the Bengali : thereby they lose whatever they have of rhythm and melody. I do not think that prose poems or spiritual apophthegms are very difficult to construct, especially if one makes a life-work of them as Tagore has done. Some of his are fine. Years ago I read one by Tagore which has remained with me :

" Why did the lamp go out ?
I shaded it with my cloak to save it from the wind, that is
why the lamp went out."

From " The Gardener."

Tagore's prose poems have crept into the antho-logies. The Poet Laureate has included three in *The Spirit of Man*. I am not much impressed by the following : " . . . Things that I longed for in vain and things I got—let them pass. Let me truly possess the things that I ever spurned and overlooked."

Until a certain afternoon in New York I had never seen Rabindranath Tagore. If I ever framed a mental picture of him he was but another of the soft-footed, soft-voiced Swami clan who glide from India to tell an obdurate Western world of their ages-old faith, and who dodge hostesses, ever on the look-out for lions, indifferent whether they roar or whisper, so long as they are lions. An actual picture I had of him in William Rothenstein's drawing, with straggly hair, curling beard, downcast eyes, and a long, pale, thin face ; he is seated on the ground contemplating nothing visible. And of course I had seen photographs of him. He is not averse to being photographed for the decoration of his books : Tagore at Riverside, Tagore at Santa Barbara, Tagore at Salt Lake City, and so on. And I had read in the papers the purpose of his latest visit to America, which was to collect funds and to arouse interest in a university he wishes to found in India where Indian lore and philosophy will be taught, with exchange professors proceeding from America and England. A modest beginning has already been made at Bolpur, about 100 miles north-west of Calcutta. Admirers of Tagore will remember that the uniform series of his works is called " The New Bolpur Edition."

After all this preparation I approach the moment when I saw Tagore. He was advertised to lecture at the Park Theatre, New York, at 2.30 on " The

Meeting of the East and West." It was a wet, cold
afternoon, the kind of day when people of leisure
prefer to stay by their radiators. I arrived at 2.28
prepared to advance to the box office with my usual
formula : " One seat, on the aisle, please, near the
stage as possible." But I found the vestibule in a
hubbub, blocked with flushed women and girls, and
two or three business men amazed to find themselves
at a *matinée*. At the box office a voice said to me,
" Tickets all sold : stay, I can give you one in the
twelfth row of the balcony."

I wedged my way into the seat, and there I sat
hemmed in, very cross, and saying to myself, " Be
just to Tagore. It isn't his fault that he is popular
with the ladies, and that you have a bad seat." I
did not feel any better when the curtain rose dis-
closing a Broadway baronial hall, rather dim and
rather fusty. Near the footlights was a table and
on the o. p. side of it stood a painted parchment
cylindrical lamp about two feet high. Behind this
was another table, and on the p. side stood another
painted parchment cylindrical lamp, larger, about
four feet high.

Mine eyes dazzled, and I said aloud, " I don't like
it." The lady on my o. p. side murmured, " Evi-
dently, it's Indian symbolism."

" Nonsense," I cried. " You can buy those lamps
on Fifth Avenue."

" Hush, hush ! " cried all the contiguous ladies,
" hush ! "

The lights in the theatre went down, you could
have heard a fan wave, as from a door at the back of
the baronial hall emerged a gentleman in a tail coat,

the typical Introducer; but nobody troubled about him. It was his attitude we watched—his inclined head, his shrinking into the shade of the oriel window, just as the members of a Cabinet act when a President or a Prime Minister enters the room. When the Introducer was well out of the way in the oriel window inclosure, and his head and shoulders had attained their lowest droop, Tagore glided into the painted parchment cylindrical illumination, and stood erect and still, like a time-worn pillar, between the two lamps. He is over six feet tall, and he was clad in a dusky-red garment, falling from neck to feet. We call it in provincial cities of England and America a dressing-gown; but in India I have no doubt that it is the correct costume for Sir Rabindranath Tagore, Kt., cr. 1915; D.Lit. Calcutta Univ., to wear.

There he stood, illumined from behind and before, detached, remote (oh, so remote!), just as he looked (without the lighting) at the Yale-Princeton football match, which he found " unrestful." He did not move except to take from his toga a pamphlet with a blue cover, his lecture. This he held negligently, while the Introducer in a score or so of words, presented the Sage to the hushed audience.

I heard him perfectly even from my distant seat. His voice, high-pitched, monotonously musical, has carrying power, and when he lapsed into Bengali I felt that I was by Ganges, not by Hudson. He, himself, was like an apparition : he addressed us and yet he ignored us : he meandered on, passionless, plaintive, and when it was over he vanished silently from the baronial hall, ignoring us and the

U

Introducer, who again stood with bent head shrinking into the shade of the oriel window.

The matter of the lecture was all right, on the lines of the essays in his book called *Sadhana*, which I consider is Tagore's best production. He has been called the Maeterlinck of the East : it would be hard to write a poor book on such a fruitful subject as the philosophy of ancient India expressed in Matthew Arnold's—

> " The East bowed low before the blast
>   In patient, deep disdain,
>   She let the legions thunder past,
>   And plunged in thought again."

Another of Tagore's good books is his translation of the songs of fifteenth-century Kabir, who strikes me as a greater poet than Tagore. If I may so express it, there is more " bite " in Kabir, and more real profundity.

Tagore's most popular book is his *Gitanjali* or *Song Offerings*. It has an amazing introduction by W. B. Yeats, who says, " These prose translations from Rabindranath Tagore have stirred my blood as nothing has for years." I have given up trying to account for what an Irish poet will say and do. As to Tagore's plays, *The Post Office* and *Sacrifice*, which have been received with polite respect in London, I suspend judgment.

It is my custom when writing around an author to inflict questions upon my friends. " What do you think of Tagore ? " I asked an artist.

He ruminated a minute, then answered, " I met him once in a country house. He was the most silent, ascetic chap I have ever come in contact with. He would sit for hours on a divan in the back hall lost in contemplation. He got on my nerves. My hostess told me that he was a great man. I never doubted it until you began talking about him."

XLIX. A. B. WALKLEY

I TURNED my back on Niagara Falls and opened *Playhouse Impressions* by A. B. Walkley at the chapter headed "*Hedda Gabler*, Vaudeville Theatre, London, April, 1891."

The rhythmic thunder of the Falls is not unpleasant, but I did not want to look at the cascade longer. I preferred A. B. Walkley. At that choice I smiled. The contrast between A. B. W. and Niagara Falls is so sufficient. It was quite easy to ignore the Falls. All I did was to turn round my rocker on the hotel balcony, compose myself snugly, and read what one of the acutest, subtlest, and most amusingly cynical, and least idealistic of modern minds thought about Ibsen and the world in 1891. A. B. W. thinks the same to-day, I am sure. Such minds do not change. They become more sensitive and more perceptive; but they run on the old rails. They do not diverge into side-tracks; they never soar into the empyrean; but being compact and allusive, and intensely interested in mental impressions of the moment, they have neat and ardent communications for the trained reader.

Do you blame me for preferring Arthur Bingham Walkley to the famous Falls? I had already done my duty to them. Clad in oilskins I had gone under them, looked down upon them, been sprayed by them, and had stood on the deck of the *Maid of the*

Mist, while she thrust her audacious nose almost into the cascade, staying there some minutes panting, as if saying : " You're big, and you make a lot of noise, but I'm not afraid of you."

Moreover, fixing my eyes on a book instead of directing them to the Falls pleased me because it was stolen reading. In such reading I delight.

A book is never so interesting as when snatching at a passage in the midst of other claims.

I had brought *Playhouse Impressions* with me on this journey to study it carefully. Reading an article by this author in the London *Times* on " Coterie Criticism," quoted by the *New York Times,* I was moved to write about A. B. W. So when the hour came to take that wonderful tram-car ride down the edge of the gorge to Queenston I carried the book with me ; and I withdrew my eyes from the rapids and the whirlpool on one side, and, on the other, the most fertile fruit-belt in the Province, to read this :

" Literary criticism is not some dominie business of assigning good and bad marks, but the art of enjoying masterpieces."

Embarking on the boat for Toronto I was more concerned about not losing *Playhouse Impressions* than about my luggage. During that three hours' steam across Lake Ontario I divided my attention equally between the vast, still, reposeful waters and Mr. Walkley's alert, quick, unreposeful prose. I was not concerned either to agree or disagree with this witty, wilful, worldly author. I read him for the pleasure of perusing his polite, personal adventures among masterpieces. From *Hedda Gabler* I

turned to *Rosmersholm*, a play, I remember, that
moved me very much when I first saw it on the stage.
Was Mr. Walkley moved ? Here is the comment of
that " eclectic dilettante," A. B. W.—

" All this is very piquant, bizarre, fresh, of absorbing interest to the serious spectator, and to the
more eclectic dilettante (say the *Des Essarts* of M.
Huysmans), at least as fascinating as a Japanese curio
or the rare edition (uncut) of the *Pastissier Francoys.*"

There you have the author of *Playhouse Impressions* at his best and at his worst. But what a
triumph is his—to make me read, word for word,
a book all about thirty-year-old plays and play-
wrights. I reflected upon this as the boat steamed
across the lake ; as the lights of Toronto grew
brighter, beneath the moon and a sky of stars.

Why, you may ask, focus on a book thirty years
old ? Because it is essential Walkley. He has
published other volumes—*Frames of Mind*, 1899 ;
Dramatic Criticism, 1903 ; *Drama and Life*, 1907.
Although these volumes are extremely readable
(everything he writes is that) they do not add anything to the amiable and witty man-of-the-worldism
of *Playhouse Impressions*.

Moreover, I suspect that I have read most of the
essays contained in those books in *The Times* of
London. For years he has been the dramatic critic
of that great journal, and it is no exaggeration to say
that he has made numbers of people read his dramatic
criticism who never enter a theatre. His articles
delight me : they are so well-shaped, and so well-
written, and they always say something to the point
and wittily ; but I doubt if managers and actors

like them as well as the cultured public. He never praises when he should not praise, and he never writes " quotes," that is, sentences of uproarious appreciation that can be used in advertisements.

He is a scholar who is not afraid to play journalistically with his scholarship. He is the one dramatic critic who constantly refers to Aristotle, and occasionally to Plato and others. His knowledge of French and French dramatic history has no bounds. His master in the kind of dramatic criticism that he has introduced into England is Jules Lemaître. In the prefatory note to *Playhouse Impressions* he writes—

" I make no apology for the frequency with which that most brilliant of contemporary critics is cited in this volume. My only fear (for I cannot pretend to estimate in my own case the full extent of his influence) is lest I have not cited him often enough."

Latterly A. B. W. has been writing in *The Times*, column essays on subjects outside the theatre. These essays have a signal merit. They are always witty, always readable, and they never contain a superfluous word, if you except recondite allusions and unhackneyed French phrases, which he loves.

A. B. W. leads a double life. The division is quite proper ; but a division it is. He gives his days to official life (he may have retired, now) and his nights to the theatre.

I know him in his theatrical environment. At 7.30, on the first night of a new play, often have I seen him dining at a certain club, usually with the same set of cronies. He is a short, dapper man, something of a dandy, at any rate extremely neat, and up-to-date in his appearance. He is quiet in his manner, with an interior, somewhat bored smile, far removed from Theodore Roosevelt's jovial laugh. And I am sure that he never uses the word " bully."

Officially A. B. W. is, or was, assistant secretary to the General Post Office, and a person of importance in St. Martin's le Grand. He entered the department in 1877, and from the way he has risen, it is plain that being a disciple of Jules Lemaître does not hinder one from efficiency in a government office. He was secretary to the British delegation at the Washington Postal Congress of 1897, and he has performed other important postal duties throughout the world. Once the light of publicity flashed upon his double life. That was when a well-known Publicist complained (with his tongue in his cheek) that when he wrote to the General Post Office about the non-delivery of a letter, he received an official answer from the dramatic critic of *The Times*.

He has also seen himself on the stage. That was in the delightful comedy by George Bernard Shaw called *Fanny's First Play*. We who were present on the first night were delighted to find that the actor who played Trotter, one of the four dramatic critics in the play, was made up to resemble Mr. A. B. Walkley, and, even if the resemblance had not been perfect, the dialogue indicated A. B. W. at every point, even to his partiality for Aristotle. In the review of *Fanny's First Play* in *The Times* the next morning Mr. Walkley treated the personality aloofly, allusively and quite in the Jules Lemaître manner. When the play was published the incorrigible Bernard Shaw announced that Mr. Trotter had forgiven him beforehand, and had assisted the actor in his make-up.

It is pleasant for us ordinary people to watch such gambols; and after all this excitement, it is a relief to learn from *Who's Who* that Mr. Walkley's recreation is—gardening.

L. ISRAEL ZANGWILL

I KNEW him first as a humorist, that is, as the editor of *Ariel*, one of the many weekly, serio-comic journals that have tried to carve a slice of the popularity of *Punch*, or create a new public for the facetious, the ironic, and the pathetic. That was years ago. *Ariel* has long disappeared, and I have entirely forgotten the nature of its contents. But I clearly remember that Israel Zangwill was editor, and that the young, literary Bohemians of that day regarded him as a coming man, and quoted his paragraphs, storyettes, and jokes that appeared, I suppose, in *Ariel*.

"I've never seen such black hair as he's got," said one of these literary Bohemians, many years ago, " or such energy. Of course he's a Jew, one of the best, and he's frightfully in earnest about his race. Odd, isn't it, that two Jews—he and Solomon, the painter, should be in the running for great success in literature and painting."

No one will deny that Israel Zangwill has achieved great literary success, not unqualified, for it took him some time to realize, and he does not quite realize it yet, that his gift to the world lies in his interpretations of his own race and their ideals ; and his own large ideals worked out in his plays, and in such small, but significant books as the reprint of his lecture on *The Principle of Nationalities*.

I admit that he is a humorist, but humour is a branch of the Zangwill tree, not the tree itself. He it was who called Izaak Walton " The Judicious Hooker." That alone calls him to a niche in the Temple of Humour.

But in the *Ariel* days, before and after those lively times, it was as a kind of humorist that he strove to enter the literary fortress. Indeed, I believe that he was once included among the exponents of " the New Humour," and readers of his early books, *The Premier and the Painter*, 1888, *The Bachelors' Club*, 1891, *The Old Maids' Club*, 1892, may recall that in those volumes there are consistent attempts at facetious expression.

Recently I have re-read two of his later novels—*The Master*, published in 1895, and *The Mantle of Elijah* in 1900. I read them as a duty : as a pleasure I would never have reached the last page of either of them. The narratives do not hold me, and I feel that, *au fond*, he is really as much of a stranger to the characters as his readers are. He is out of his element in writing about a Prime Minister, a Great Painter, and a Lady of Breeding. Yet I once knew a man who raved about *The Master*. I find it intolerably long, and the final analysis of the Great Painter and the description of his pictures is merely sentimental.

With *Jinny the Carrier*, Mr. Zangwill broke a novel-writing silence of more than twenty years, and I, whose time is fully occupied, hesitate to begin this conscientious tale, which is twice as long as the ordinary novel, and which moves slowly in an Essex village in the leisurely days of the middle

nineteenth century. Mr. Zangwill likes tortoise
novels. I do not. I prefer the method of Miss Zona
Gale in *Miss Lulu Butt*.

At this point the reader may say : " Well, if
you do not like his novels and his semi-humorous
books, why write about Israel Zangwill ? " Well,
recently, he was brought vividly to my mind through
reading a very remarkable article by the Rev.
Samuel W. Purvis on " The Jew in History." When
I had finished it, I sat back in my chair, and recalled
my debt to Israel Zangwill for his interpretations of
the Jewish people. Those books—*Children of the
Ghetto, Ghetto Tragedies, Ghetto Comedies*, and
above all *Dreamers of the Ghetto*—are the real
work of his life. In them he moves spaciously,
with love and insight : in them I feel that he is
writing from his heart, not from his head, as in the
novels.

This versatile Jewish man of letters, son of Moses
Zangwill, who settled in England in 1848; who is
self-educated ; who, through his own efforts, climbed
the educational ladder and became B.A. of London ;
who is now President of the International Jewish
Territorial Organization, wrote in *Dreamers of the
Ghetto* a book that must always remain a noble and
intimate record of a great race—a prose poem. I
have preserved what Henley wrote about *Dreamers
of the Ghetto*. He said : " Here, I take it—here, so
it seems to me—is that rarest of rare things, a *book*.
As I have said, I do not wholly believe in it. But it
is a book ! It goes far to explain the Jew. It is,
in fact, a Jew of something akin to genius upon
Jewry—the unchangeable quantity. And I feel that

the reading of it has widened my horizon, and given me much to perpend."

Of his plays some of them are in the category of his semi-humorous novels ; but the three that count are *The Melting Pot, The War God* and *The Next Religion*. To these I may add *The Cock-Pit*. *The Next Religion* was forbidden public representation by the British censor, one of those acts that bring the office of the Lord Chamberlain, which licenses plays, into ridicule. As Mr. Zangwill justly observes in the Preface to the printed edition of the play—" The notion that the susceptibilities of any particular sect have to be protected by the State is opposed to the constitutional right of free speech, and seems to rest on an assumption that those likely to be offended are driven into the theatre as the Jews of the Roman Ghetto were driven into the church to be shocked by sermons."

Happily *The Melting Pot* can be freely acted. It is almost a great play ; perhaps it is a great play. I have seen it performed, and I have read, and re-read it ; particularly the Appendices, and the Afterword, that interest me as much as the play itself. I have an idea that if Mr. Zangwill were to take *The Melting Pot* in hand again, prune it, simplify it, and develop its vital parts, *The Melting Pot*, like Drinkwater's *Abraham Lincoln*, might be shaped into a play that will always hold the boards in America from one year's end to another.

His fertile pen has run easily into many fields, for he has much to say, so much, that he does not pay such close attention, as he might, to the manner of saying it. There is *Without Prejudice*, good journalism

from the *Pall Mall Magazine* and other quarters;
there is *Italian Fantasies*, good travel writing; there
is *The War for the World*, good militant, arm-chair
war-talk; there is his book of *Poems*—good verses.
These are all above the average. But it is by
Dreamers of the Ghetto and *The Melting Pot* that he
will live : these are essential Zangwill, the tree itself,
not a branch.

THE END